The Erotic Traveler

SIR RICHARD BURTON

The Erotic Traveler

EDITED BY EDWARD LEIGH

BARNES
&NOBLE
BOOKS
NEW YORK

This edition published by Barnes & Noble, Inc.,
by arrangement with G.P. Putnam's Sons.

1993 Barnes & Noble Books

ISBN 1-56619-110-6

Printed and bound in the United States of America

M 9 8 7 6 5 4 3 2 1

Contents

1. Early Life

Richard Francis Burton was born on March 19, 1821, the first of a family of three. His father, Lieutenant Colonel Joseph Netterville Burton, was a recently retired army officer of firm opinions, forthright speech, and a disinclination to stay in one place for any length of time. The first of these characteristics, which like the third was inherited in full measure by his son, had cost him his career. He had refused to testify against Queen Caroline when, in 1820, she was called before the House of Lords to answer charges of adultery. After a long trial the "Pains and Penalties" Bill, designed to deprive the Queen of her rank and to dissolve her marriage, was abandoned; but Colonel Burton's insubordination was not forgiven. On the orders of the Duke of Wellington he was retired on half pay. Fortunately his wife, neé Martha Baker, had come to him well dowered: and even if Colonel Burton was unable to touch the capital of his wife's inheritance, he was able to enjoy a fuller life than would have been possible on a colonel's half pay.

Richard's travel's began at a very early age. Soon after

he was born, the family moved across the Channel to Tours, on the Loire, where a sister and then a brother followed Richard into the world.

The children's education was desultory, discipline almost nonexistent. The older they got, the wilder Richard and his brother became. Before he was ten Richard had come to the conclusion that truth and honor were in no way connected, and he was behaving in a way that today would be regarded as unabashed juvenile delinquency. Serious though the hooliganism was becoming, it was the political situation that caused the family to return to England; and it was the need for some sort of education for the boys that saw the family settled temporarily in Richmond, Surrey, and the boys enrolled in a school run by a Rev. Charles Delafosse. It was not a very good school. When Richard caught measles there, the Colonel, who had greatly missed his boar hunting, felt justified in taking his sons away and in moving his family back to France.

Only a year was spent at Blois before Colonel Burton decided to move to Italy, around which this restless family moved for several years. As Mr. Byron Farwell writes in his admirable biography of Richard Burton, "the Colonel's solution to every crisis was to move." In the Burton family, crises were not uncommon.

This peripatetic existence, during which Richard and Edward suffered little discipline and generally behaved very badly, gave them both a sound knowledge of Italian and a range of experience far wider than most men gain in a lifetime. In Naples, where there was a cholera epidemic, the brothers found it amusing to dress up in old clothes and to spend the night loading bodies of the victims onto the dead carts. In Naples too the boys discovered a brothel within sight of their house. They visited it, and then began a correspondence with the prostitutes, their

8

passionate letters eliciting extremely bawdy replies. Richard was then sixteen years of age.

When the correspondence was discovered the Colonel was furious and reacted in his usual way. He moved his family first to Provence, and then to the pure air of the Basses Pyrenées at Pau. But his sons had an eye for excitement, and they soon discovered a band of smugglers with whom they would spend the evenings drinking, singing and enjoying the company of girls. They took up smoking, and indulged in a series of love affairs with English girls whose parents had come to the resort.

In 1840, after sundry crises and the consequent moves, Colonel Burton decided that his sons should have the advantages of a university education—particularly as, against all the evidence, he wanted them to go into the Church. So in the autumn of that year Richard went up to Trinity College, Oxford. His accomplishments—a knowledge of the world, of French and Italian in various dialects, of chess and of fencing—were not exactly those required by a classical university. Of Greek and Latin he had little, of religion none. His whole upbringing had established in him a feeling that it was right that he should be allowed to do anything he liked, and had encouraged in him, as a corollary, an almost total disdain for authority. It can readily be imagined, therefore, that he and the university were not very suited to each other. "I was always of the opinion," he once wrote, "that a man proves his valor by doing exactly what he likes." He reacted to the university by doing just this. He fenced, he formed a liaison with a pretty gypsy girl, he began to teach himself Arabic, he argued against his professors about the Latin pronunciation then in vogue. Such behavior did not endear him to the university authorities, and it is probable that they eagerly seized upon the excuse to send him down when he and some cronies attended a horse race to which students had been forbidden to go. Richard Burton was the only one so irrevocably disciplined.

He now had to decide how he was going to make a living. His mind was soon made up. England was far too stuffy and dull: he would join the Army in India as an officer of the Honourable East India Company. Normally, commissions with the Company were not for purchase, but it so happened that following a disastrous defeat of the Army in Afghanistan the Honourable Company was in need of men. For the sum of £500 Richard Burton became an ensign in the Bombay Native Infantry. He immediately set about learning Hindustani.

2. India

In June 1842, Richard Burton, tall, dark, with a drooping moustache, sailed from Gravesend and, after a voyage of four months, arrived in Bombay. There he at once set about investigating English society and Indian prostitutes (he disliked the former and did not record his views on the latter) and continued to work at Hindustani and Arabic, using a system of learning that he had developed himself. After a few weeks he was ordered to join his regiment, the 18th Regiment of Bombay Native Infantry, at Baroda.

He found it engaged in normal peacetime pursuits, the Afghan disaster having been avenged by Lord Ellenborough. There was a certain amount of drill, some cockfighting, pigsticking, riding and runting, and Burton indulged in these like any other junior officer. But he also spent up to twelve hours a day on his language studies, and soon discovered the advantages (in this and in other fields of learning) of possessing a native mistress. After six months he sat the official examination in Hindustani and passed out top: after another five months he did the same with Gujarati.

At the beginning of 1844 the 18th Regiment was ordered to the province of Sind (in what is now West Pakistan), recently conquered by Sir Charles Napier. Burton immediately set about learning Marathi, and again came first in the official examination. Attached to the Sind Survey, whose headquarters were at Karachi, he now became deeply involved in local Indian life, every facet of which became of absorbing interest to him. He had a passion for experience, and for knowledge for its own sake. His approach to it was unemotional, uninvolved, scientific in its close observance of detail. He had a prodigious memory, and a genuinely inquiring mind that was limited only by certain prejudices and *idées fixes* that remained unaltered throughout his life.

In his search for knowledge of native customs and native life, he disguised himself as a native and opened three shops where he sold a few goods and obtained a great and varied store of information on religion, magic, sexual practices, aphrodisiacs and many other subjects. Much of the information gathered at this period by the twenty-four-year-old junior officer was recorded in notebooks, to appear in 1851 in a book entitled *Sindh, and the Races that Inhabit the Valley of the Indus; with Notices of the Topography and History of the Province.*

It was in this book that he first expressed the view which he was to repeat continually in other books throughout his life, that women in "warm, damp countries lying close to mountains" are more passionate than men, while the reverse is true in cold countries. Upon what evidence, direct or indirect, he based this proposition is not recorded: he was never afraid to convert dubious theories into categorical statements. But whether they were passionate or not, Burton held the women of Sind in low regard:

Throughout the Moslem world, the two great points of honor are bravery and chastity in women. Judged by this test the Sindis occupy a low place in the scale of Oriental nations. Under the native rule, however, several instances of honorable conduct (Orientally speaking) are quoted in favor of the Sindis. One of the reigning clan, Fatteh Khan Talpur, was slain by a Langho, or common musician, who detected him in an intrigue with his wife. A Shikari (sweeper), one of the vilest of classes in Sind, ripped up with a sickle the belly of Ahmed Khan Numdani, one of the chief Sardars, for the same reason. There are two causes in the province why the punishment for adultery was made so severe: in the first place the inadequacy of the Koranic law; secondly, the physical peculiarities of the people. As is often the case in warm and damp countries, lying close to mountains, the amativeness of the female here appears to be stronger than that of the male. We find, accordingly, that in all the vernacular books the fair sex is represented as more worthless in Sind than in any other part of the world. It is amusing to observe the virulence of abuse with which the ladies are assailed, especially when the reason is duly considered.

In point of personal appearance the Sindi woman is of fairer complexion and finer features and form than those of Western India; the latter, however, are superior in grace and delicacy of make. Toward the north of our province there is a considerable portion of personal beauty, especially among the females of the higher classes. Their education is much neglected. Few can read, and still fewer can write, their own language: to peruse the Koran without understanding a word of it is considered a feat and in a large town not more than four or five women would be able to spell through a Persian letter. Still there are female teachers who, when required, can educate a girl; their chief occupations, however, are reading billet-doux of absent lovers, and inditing answers to the same. The usual Moslem prejudice against female education is strong in Sind. All are agreed upon one point, viz., that their women are quite bad enough, without enlarging their ideas and putting such weapons as pens into their hands. In manners the Sandi female wants the mildness of the Indian and the vivacity of the Afghan and Persian. She is rather grave and sedate than otherwise in society, and is not so much at ease in it owing to the want of Hammans and frequent social intercourse. She is fond of play and can cheat with formidable dexterity. The chief games are Pachis, Cards and Cowries (thrown like dice) and the excitement caused by them is so great that violent quarrels frequently occur, even when no wagers are laid. Sindi women are most indecent in their language, especially in abuse; they have very few expressions peculiar to their sex, but deliberately select the worst words used by the men. They are fond of drinking liqueurs and the different preparations of hemp: intoxication is always the purpose of their potations. Many of them take snuff and almost all smoke Sukho (tobacco) in the Hookah. Their other amusements are dressmaking, the toilette, visits and intrigues. The preparations for the latter occupations throughout the country are rather extensive.

Burton then goes on to describe the clothes worn by the women of Sind, explaining that unmarried girls usually dress in red colors, while old women and widows wear white. He describes the veil and the "Cholo," a shift opening in front, and sleeves reaching down to the elbows:

Under the shift a bit of cloth called Kanjari, Choli, or Gaj, conceals the bosom; when it passes round the sides like a bodice and is fastened behind, its name is Puthi. This advisable article of dress is very often omitted in Sind—a fact which may in some measure account for the pendant shape which the bosom assumes even in young women after a first or second child.*

It did not strike Burton as odd that in a country in which female amativeness was so strong there should be any need for magic or talismans to increase it:

The practice of magic in Sind, as in the East generally, consists of talismans and different ceremonies for inspiring love, causing hatred, destroying enemies, raising oneself in the world, escaping mysterious dangers (such as the evil eye, or the praise of a foe), averting and curing pain, disease, barrenness and abortion, securing wishes, and detecting thieves. . . .

The following are short specimens of some of the most peculiar talismans:

When a man desires to excite love in a woman, he selects seven large cloves on the seventeenth day of the month, and recites the following prayer seven times over each of them:

*Burton adds in a footnote: Perhaps there may be some physiological reason for this peculiarity. It is observable among the nations living between the Caspian and India, as the Persians, Afghans, Belochis and Sindis. It is found in Cashmir, but it is not general in Hindustan.

O cloves! O cloves! ye are truly good;
She that is bound by the cloves can never remain
away from me!
To whomsoever, after this recitation, I give the clove,
She, falling and rising (i.e. eagerly), will come to me.

The amorist then contrives that the woman may eat the cloves, and feels assured of success.

Salt is pressed into the service of Cupid in the following manner. On the first Sunday of the month the lover recites these lines seven times over a handful of salt:

O salt! O thou salt one! thou essence of the seven seas!
O certain person (naming the woman)—eat my salt, and kiss my feet.

The reciter then dissolves the salt in water and drinks it; the consequence of which is that the other party falls violently in love with him.

Should the lady resist these measures, the disappointed lover becomes desperate, and proceeds to extremes. From the harmless specimen subjoined, it will be evident that passion frequently gets the better of delicacy. Agathu chinnanu, or "breaking the trowser string," is done by reciting a charm over seven or nine threads of raw cotton, spun by a girl not yet betrothed. The bits are then rolled up and knotted seven times; after which the lady is duly warned of the punishment of disdain. Should she persevere in cruelty, one of the knots is opened, and by a curious coincidence, the string which confines the fair one's trousers, breaks of itself and leaves that garment unsupported. This operation is repeated until she yields; an event which, says the book that details the plan, may soon be expected.

The system of philters and amatory talismans is probably borrowed by the Moslems from the Hindoos, to whom it has long been known by the name of Washikaran. It is to the advantage of all parties to support the idea. The magician gains money by teaching his craft, the fair sex have a valid excuse when detected in a grave delinquency, and the husbands are consoled by the reflection that the chastity of their spouses could yield to none but preternatural influence. Belief in it is almost universal; as a proof of which, no woman would allow a lock of hair to be taken even by her husband, for fear of the power it might give him. The art has a bad name, and it is probably with reason that the people assert that adepts in it generally meet with accidents. It is not, however, used for illicit love only; there are many semireligious charms, containing texts of the Koran, to be recited by those who desire to marry, or who wish to retain the affections of a wife.

Since in some instances the affection of a wife depends upon the virility of the husband, any man who feared to lose his wife owing to a lessening, either imagined or real, of his sexual powers would inevitably seek some aphrodisiacal philter or talisman. Burton must have seen them on sale in the bazaars, and he had certainly read of their huge variety, but nowhere does he write at length upon them.

The subject of aphrodisiacs [he writes in Supplemental vol. iii, p. 133] would fill a small library: almost every medical treatise ends in a long disquisition upon fortifiers, provocatives, etc. We may briefly divide them into three great classes. The first is medicinal, which may be either external or internal. The second is the mechanical, such as scarification, flagellation, and the application of insects as practiced by certain savage races. There is a veritable Joe Miller of an old Brahmin whose young wife always insisted, each time before he possessed her, upon his being stung by a bee in certain parts. The third is magical, superstitious and so forth.

As an example of the first type of aphrodisiac Burton would probably have given ambergris, which he states is found in lumps weighing several pounds upon the Zanzibar coast. This substance, he writes (Vol. vi, p. 60) "is sold at a high price, being held a potent aphrodisiac." He goes on to explain that it is drunk in coffee. "A small hollow is drilled in the bottom of the cup, and the coffee is poured upon the bit of ambergris it contains," notes Burton, who then details the way in which expert coffee-servants prepare and serve the brew.

That magical sexual stimulants are not always what they seem is evidenced by a curious little story Burton relates in a footnote in Supplemental vol. iii. p. 182: He claims it occurred in Paris "during the debauched days of the Second Empire."

Before a highly "fashionable" assembly of men appeared a youth in fleshings who sat down upon a stool, bared his pudenda and closed his eyes when, by "force of fancy," erection and emission took place. But presently it was suspected and proved that the stool was hollow and admitted from below a hand whose titillating fingers explained the phenomenon.

Nevertheless, Burton did not deride the magical aphrodisiac, as is shown by his sympathetic footnote to the entertaining and rather sad little story (Supplemental vol. iv. p. 257) of Fruiterer "whose prickle would not stand to the handmaid as was the wont thereof. So he cried, 'Verily, this is a wondrous business.' Then the girl fell to rubbing it up and to toying therewith, her object being to stablish erection. But the article in question grew not and remained limp, whereupon she said, 'O my lord, Allah increase the progress of thy pego!' Thereupon she arose and opened a bag wherefrom she drew out kerchiefs and dried aromatic herbs such as are scattered upon corpses; and she also brought a gugglet of water. Presently she fell to washing the prickle as it were a dead body, and after bathing it she shrouded it with a kerchief: then she cried upon her women and they all bewept the untimely fate of his yard which was still clothed in the kerchief."

These comical measures, writes Burton were taken by 'Miss Lucy' in order to charm away the Evil Eye which had fascinated the article in question. Such temporary impotence in a vigorous man, which results from an exceptional action of the brain and the nervous system, was called in old French *Nouement des aiguillettes* (i.e., point-tying, the points which fastened the haut-de-chausses or hose to the jerkin, and its modern equivalent would be to 'button up the flap'). For its cure, the *'Déliement des aiguilettes'* see Davenport *Aphrodisiacs* p. 36, and the French translation of *The Perfumed Garden,* ch. xvii, pp. 251-253. The Moslem heal such impotence by the usual simples, but the girl in the text adopts a moral course of treatment which buries the dead parts in order to resurrect them. A friend of mine, a young and vigorous officer, was healed by a similar process. He had carried off a sergeant's wife, and the husband lurked about the bungalow in order to shoot him, a copper cap being found under the window, hence a state of nervousness which induced perfect impotence. He applied to the regimental surgeon, happily a practiced hand, and was gravely supplied with pills and a draught; his diet was carefully regulated and he was ordered to sleep by the woman but by no means to touch her for ten days. On the fifth he came to his adviser with a sheepish face and told him he had not wholly followed the course prescribed, as last night he had suddenly—by the blessing of the draught and the pills—recovered and had given palpable evidence of his pristine vigor. The surgeon deprecated such proceeding until the patient should have had full benefit of his drugs—bread pills and cinnamon-water.

That the "system of philters and amatory talismans" was not altogether effective in inducing compliance in the loved one is suggested by the presence in Karachi of seven procuresses:

For instance, in the small town of Kurrachee (Karachi) there are no less than seven Kutni (procuresses), three of them Hindoos and four Moslems. The custom is to go to the old woman's house and there sit down. She closes the door that no stranger may enter, offers water to drink, with a pipe of tobacco, and at the same time inquires the name and other particulars of her visitor. After much preparatory conversation, the man discloses his object, and requests the Kutni to procure him the means of meeting the fair dame. The old woman at first positively refuses, on account of many alleged difficulties: then she reluctantly agrees to undertake a trial, but insists upon the expense, and finally after receiving her Lawazimo (the technical name for the small present of a few annas made on such occasions) and making a formal bargain for what she is to get in case of success, dismisses her employer with many promises. She afterwards, if properly paid, allows the parties to meet at her house, and manages their different interviews. The employment is a lucrative but not a safe one, the Kutni being perpetually exposed to the resentment of injured husbands who sometimes use the stick without remorse. These old hags are accused of many actions of gross villainy, such as administering narcotics, preventives and abortives, and practicing unholy rites, in order to subjugate the wells of their victims. Probably their promises and flattering tongues are the natural magic which works such wonders. Women in Sind are devotedly fond of flattery, and find no description of it too gross or ridiculous. Their chief inducements to intrigue, besides passion and want of employment, are avarice and pride. Curious to say (among Moslems) it is no small honor for a woman to boast of her intimacy with some great man, such as a Kardar or a Kazi. In intrigue the Sindi woman is far more daring than her Indian sister, though much inferior, when there is real danger, to the Persian or Afghan. Some cases of considerable audacity are quoted. For instance, the wives of Mir Mohammed, one of the reigning family, had the boldness, it is said, to introduce into the palace by means of an old woman a young Beloch dressed in female clothes. The lover in his attempt to escape, when he found a longer stay impossible, fell from the roof, broke his leg, and was secretly put to death by the Darban (guards). The ladies escaped all the evil consequences which might be expected from so barefaced an affair.

With so many passionate women, with love talismans to be purchased and with procuresses available for employment, it might be thought that love itself might not have been a very salable commodity. Yet prostitutes not only existed; they were (as Burton writes in his usual categorical way) of two kinds:

Prostitutes in Sind are of two kinds. The Rangeli, or Khobli, is a low courtesan of the Jatki race, from the districts of Ubho and Jhangsiyal. They inhabit villages close to the main roads, and support themselves and the males by the contributions of travelers. The sum usually paid is from three to four pice [four pice-one] annal, besides which the visitor is expected to make a present of hemp or tobacco. Some of these women have very fine features and forms, particularly in early youth. The debauched life they lead soon makes them look old. In spite of their depravity they are very attentive to the duties of their religion, and never object to devote a certain portion of their ill-gotten gains to the support of a mosque and its officiating Mulla.

Another and a more respectable class is the Kanyari, who, like the Nautch girl of India, generally unites the occupation of dancing with the more immoral part of her trade. An individual of this order has, generally speaking, her own house, is often married to a musician, who attends her at the different dances, and lives comfortably enough. Nautches frequently take place at sacred spots, and invariably on occasions of marriage and other feasts. At such times it is customary for the master of the house to give two or three rupees to the dancing girl when she comes round to collect money; all the visitors present are expected to do the same, under pain of being reputed miserly in the extreme. The sum thus raised in one night is often considerable. A first-rate Nautch girl expects about one hundred rupees for an evening's performance; the inferior ones take as little as ten or twelve. Some of these Kanyari strive to attract attention by fixing the price of their favors extremely high. They calculate upon and often succeed in finding amongst the natives, despite their usual parsimony, fools who court the celebrity of wasting their money in this species of debauchery. On one occasion, I heard of a respectable merchant giving as much as two hundred rupees for a single visit. As the Kanyari grows old, she is compelled, if she has been extravagant in youth, to depend upon the exertions of her daughters or her slave girls. When money is saved, it is invariably laid out in ornaments and jewels, which, as in India, are handed down from parent to child till urgent necessity compels the family to part with them. This practice, which occasionally collects several hundred pounds' worth of articles easily robbed, in a poor country is often dangerous; many murders have been caused by it. Under the native governments, the Kanyari used to pay a certain annual sum for permission to exercise her craft. They were, however, only tolerated, not encouraged as in India; no respectable woman was permitted to degrade herself by joining the class, and to the honor of the Sindis it must be said that, like the Arabs, they considered visiting the houses of prostitutes a disgrace to the visitor—not the person visited. The Kanyari is, generally speaking, well dressed and clean in her person, she seldom drinks more than other women, and, like the lower orders of the frail sisterhood, is scrupulously obedient to the injunctions of her religious teachers.

In Burton's view feminine immorality in Sind had been kept in check only by the use of the saber, by which he meant the practice of Sindi husbands of chopping off the heads of erring wives. When Sir Charles Napier forbade this long-established custom and even hanged a man who had so disciplined an unfaithful wife, he upset what had been regarded as the natural order of things and provided no substitute sanction. According to Burton the result was just what might have been expected: married women became so immoral that they threatened the livelihood of the prostitutes. He was pleased to be able to make this point in a footnote:

A new class has lately appeared, composed of women

23

who are half respectable, half prostitutes; they devote themselves to Europeans and the Sepoys. At Hyderabad, the courtesans have complained that their occupation was gone, in consequence of the loose conduct of the married women.

Burton never changed his view on this matter. In a footnote to the "Twenty-ninth Night" *Arabian Nights,* vol. 1, p. 298), he wrote concerning the women of Cairo:

The Cairenes have always been held exceedingly debauched. . . . With civilization, which objects to the good old remedy, the sword, they became worse; and the Kazi's court is crowded with would-be divorcees. Under English rule the evil has reached its acme because it goes unpunished: in the avenues of the new Isma'iliyah Quarter, inhabited by Europeans, women, even young women, will threaten to expose their persons unless they receive "bakhshish." It was the same in Sind when husbands were assured that they would be hanged for cutting down adulterous wives: at once after its conquest the women broke loose; and in 1843-50, if a young officer sent to the bazaar for a girl, half a dozen would troop to his quarters. Indeed more than once the professional prostitutes threatened to memorialize Sir Charles Napier because the "modest women," the "ladies," were taking the bread out of their mouths. The same was the case at Kabul of Afghanistan in the old war of 1840; and here the women had more excuse, the husbands being notable sodomites as the song has it:

The worth of slit the Afghan knows;
The worth of hole the Kabul-man.

Furthermore, in Volume X of the *Arabian Nights* there

occurs the story of Ma'aruf the Cobbler, who sadly mis-treated his wife Fatimah. The Kazi, who was a benevolent man, "made peace between them, saying, 'O wife, obey thy husband; and thou, O man, deal kindly with her.' " This unexceptionable and indeed praiseworthy remark drew from Burton the following footnote:

This is a true picture of the leniency with which women were treated in the Kazi's court at Cairo; and the effect was simply deplorable. I have noted that matters have grown even worse since the English occupation, for his-tory repeats herself; and the same was the case in Afghan-istan and in Sind. We govern too much in these matters, which should be directed not changed, and too little in other things, especially in exacting respect for the con-querors from the conquered.

If heterosexual sex was available in Sind at a range of prices, so also was homosexual sex. Here, though, differ-ent criteria affected the price, uncastrated boys being twice as expensive as eunuchs for reasons that Burton explained in one of the many footnotes which he so liberally scat-tered throughout his books (and which are usually better written than the main text).

In 1845 it was reported to Sir Charles Napier that there existed in Karachi some male brothels. Burton wrote later that he was asked "indirectly to make inquiries and to report on the subject," though how he was asked "in-directly" is not explained. Being the man he was he prob-ably took it upon himself to investigate the phenomenon as a result of a remark made by Sir Charles and overheard by Burton or by a fellow officer. But however it came about, he took the investigation seriously and pursued it with the thoroughness he applied to any subject that inter-ested him.

Disguising himself as a merchant, Mirza Abdullah of Bushiri, and accompanied by a Munshi or teacher, he located the brothels and visited them time and time again until he knew everything about the system of male prostitution. He then wrote a full and detailed report for Sir Charles Napier, intending it for his eyes only. Unfortunately Sir Charles resigned in 1847, and the report was forwarded, along with other documents, to the Government in Bombay. It can be well imagined that a long account of pederasty in Sind by a junior officer would not be likely to assist his promotion; and indeed it seems to have been this report that ruined his career in the Indian Army, even though the recommendation for his summary dismissal was not accepted. The blow, however, was delayed.

In his later travels and in his wide reading in many literatures Richard Burton continued to gather information on pederasty. All this he collected into a long essay that became sub-section D of the famous "Terminal Essay" that forms the bulk of Volume X of *The Arabian Nights*. Since the essay has its origins in the male brothels of Karachi in 1845, it is quoted now as if belonging to this stage of Burton's travels.

The execrable race of male prostitutes first came before me by a chance of earlier life. In 1845, when Sir Charles Napier had conquered and annexed Sind, despite a fraction (mostly venal) which sought favor with the now defunct "Court of Directors to the Honourable East India Company," the veteran began to consider his conquest with a curious eye. It was reported to him that Karachi, a townlet of some two thousand souls and distant not more than a mile from camp, supported no less than three lupanars or bordels, in which not women but boys and

26

eunuchs, the former demanding nearly a double price, lay for hire.*

Being then the only British officer who could speak Sindi, I was asked indirectly to make inquiries and to report uopn the subject; and I undertook the task on express condition that my report should not be forwarded to the Bombay Government, from whom supporters of the Conqueror's policy could expect scant favor, mercy or justice. Accompanied by a *Munshi,* Mirza Mohammed Hosayn of Shiraz, and habited as a merchant, Mirza Abdullah the Bushiri passed many an evening in the townlet, visited all the brothels and obtained the fullest details which were duly dispatched to Government House. But the "Devil's Brother" presently quitted Sind leaving in his office my unfortunate official: this found its way with sundry other reports to Bombay and produced the expected result. A friend in the Secretariat informed me that my summary dismissal from the service had been formally proposed by one of Sir Charles Napier's successors, whose decease compels me to spare the dead. But this excess so outraged modesty was not allowed.

Subsequent inquiries in many and distant countries enabled me to arrive at the following conclusions:

*Burton's footnote explains this price differential in the following terms: This detail especially excited the veteran's curiosity. The reason proved to be that the scrotum of an unmutilated boy could be used as a kind of bridle for directing the movement of the animal. I find nothing of the kind mentioned in the Sotadical literature of Greece and Rome; although the same cause might be expected everywhere to have the same effect. But in Mirabeau (Kadhésch) a grand seigneur of modern times when his confidential manservant proposes to provide him with women instead of boys, exclaims, "Women! Pah, it's as though you served a roast leg of mutton, with nothing to hold the bone while I carved it!"

1. There exists what I shall call a "Sotadic Zone," bounded westwards by the northern shore of the Mediterranean (N. Lat. 43°) and by the southern (N. Lat. 30°). Thus, the depth would be 780 to 800 miles including meridional France, the Iberian Peninsula, Italy and Greece, with the coast regions of Africa from Morocco to Egypt.

2. Running eastward the Sotadic Zone narrows, embracing Asia Minor, Mesopotamia and Chaldea, Afghanistan, Sind, the Punjab and Kashmir.

3. In Indo-China, the belt begins to broaden, enfolding China, Japan and Turkistan.

4. It then embraces the South Sea Islands, and the New World where, at the time of its discovery, Sotadic love was, with some exceptions, an established racial institution.

5. Within the Sotadic Zone, the vice is popular and endemic, held at the worst to be a mere peccadillo, while the races to the north and south of the limits here defined practice it only sporadically amid the opprobium of their fellows who, as a rule, are physically incapable of performing the operation and look upon it with the liveliest disgust.

Before entering into topographical details concerning pederasty, which I hold to be geographical and climatic, not racial, I must offer a few considerations of its cause and origin. We must not forget that the love of boys has its noble, sentimental side. The Platonists and pupils of the academy, followed by the Sufis or Moslem Gnostics, held such affection, pure and ardent, to be the *beau idéal* which united in man's soul the creature with the Creator. Professing to regard youths as the most cleanly and beautiful objects in this phenomenal world, they declared that by loving and extolling the *chef-d'œuvre,* corporeal and intellectual, of the Demiurgus, disinterestedly and without

28

any admixture of carnal sensuality, they are paying the most fervent adoration to the cause in action. They add that such affection, passing as it does the love of women, is far less selfish than fondness for and admiration to the other sex which, however innocent, always suggest sexuality; and Easterns add that the devotion of the moth to the taper is purer and more fervent than the Bulbul's love for the rose. Among the Greeks of the best ages the system of boy favorites was advocated on considerations of morals and politics. The lover undertook the education of the beloved through precept and example, while the two were conjoined by a tie stricter than the fraternal. Hieronymus, the Peripatetic, strongly advocated it because the vigorous disposition of youth and the confidence engendered by their association often led to the overthrow of tyrannies. Socrates declared that "a most valiant army might be composed of boys and their lovers; for that of all men they would be most ashamed to desert one another". And even Virgil, despite the foul flavor of "The shepherd Corydon lusted after the beautiful boy Alexis." could write:

Nisus in chaste love of the boy.

The only physical cause for the practice which suggests itself to me (that must be owned to be purely conjectural) is that within the Sotadic Zone there is a blending of the masculine and feminine temperaments, a crasis which elsewhere occurs only sporadically. Hence the male effeminacy whereby the man becomes passive as well as active, and the woman a tribade, a votary of mascula Sappho, Queen of Frictrices or Rubbers.* Prof. Mantegazza claims

*In two footnotes Burton expands these references as follows: "Mascula," from the priapiscus, the overdevelopment of the clitoris ... which enabled her to play the man. Sappho

(612 B.C.) has been *retoillée* like Mary Stuart, La Brinvilliers, Mary Antoinette and a host of feminine names which have a savor not of sanctity.

"Queen of Frictrices": hence to Lesbianize and tribassare; the former applied to the love of woman for woman and the latter to its means whereby it is expressed: this is either natural, as friction of the labia and insertion of the clitoris when unusually developed; or artificial by means of the fascinum, the artificial penis; the cat's foot, the banana-fruit and a multitude of other substitutes.

And elsewhere in a further footnote (*Arabian Nights,* vol. 11, p. 234, he provides the following gloss on tribadism:

The Moslem harem is a great school for this "Lesbian (which I should call Atossan) love"; but the motive of the practice lies deeper. As among men the mixture of the feminine with the masculine temperament leads to sodomy, so the reverse makes women prefer their own sex. These tribades are mostly known by peculiarities of form and features, hairy cheeks and upper lips, gruff voices, hircine odor and the large projecting clitoris with erectile powers known to the Arabs as "bazar," hence Tabzir=circumcision or amputation of such clitoris. Burckhardt (Prov. 436) translates "Bazarah" by slut and wench. He adds "it originally signifies the labia which the Cairenes also entitle Zambúr and which are cut off in girlhood." See also Lane, Lex. s.v.; Tabzir. Both writers confuse excision of the nymphae with circumcision of the clitoris (Zambúr). Al-Siyúti (Kitab al-Izá'fi'Ilm al-Nikah) has a very interesting chapter on Sapphic venery, which is well known to Europe as proved by such works as *Gamiani,* and *Anandria ou Confessions de Mademoiselle Sappho, avec le Clef,* Lesbos, 1778. Onanism is fatally prevalent: in many harems and girls' schools tallow candles and similar succedanea are vainly forbidden and bananas when detected are cut into four as to be useless; of late years, however, China has sent some marvelous artificial phalli of stuffed bladder, horn and even caoutchouc, the latter material of course borrowed from Europe.

to have discovered the cause of this pathologic love, this perversion of the erotic sense, one of the marvelous list of amorous vagaries which deserve, not prosecution but the pitiful care of the physician and the study of the psychologist. According to him, the nerves of the rectum and the genitalia, in all cases closely connected, are abnormally so in the pathic who obtains, by intromission, the venereal orgasm which is usually sought through the sexual organs. So among women, there are tribads who can procure no pleasure except by foreign objects introduced into the backside. Hence his threefold distribution of sodomy: 1, Peripheric or anatomical, caused by an unusual distribution of the nerves and their hyperesthesia; 2, luxurious, when buttock love is preferred on account of the narrowness of the passage; and 3, the psychical. But this is evidently superficial: the question is what causes this neuropathy, this abnormal distribution and condition of the nerves?*

As Prince Bismarck finds a moral difference between the male and female races of history, so I suspect a mixed physical temperament effected by the manifold subtle influences massed together in the world climate. Something of the kind is necessary to explain the fact of this pathological love extending over the greater portion of the habitable world, without any apparent connection of race or media, from the polished Greek to the cannibal Tupi of Brazil. Walt Whitman speaks of the ashen gray faces of onanists:

*Plato (Symp.) is probably mystical when he accounts for such passions by there being in the beginning three species of humanity, men, women and men-women or androgynes. When the latter were destroyed by Zeus for rebellion, the two others were individually divided into equal parts. Hence each division seeks its other half in the same sex; the primitive man prefers men and the primitive woman women. *C'est beau*, but—is it true? . . .

31

the faded colors, the puffy features and the unwholesome complexion of the professed pederast with his peculiar cachectic expression, indescribable but once seen never forgotten which stamps the breed, and Dr. G. Adolph is justified in declaring "All confirmed pederasts recognize each other rapidly, often with a glance." This has nothing in common with the effeminacy which betrays itself in the pathic by womanly gait, regard and gesture: it is a something peculiar to itself; and the same may be said of the color and look of the young priest who honestly refrains from women and their substitutes. Dr. Tardieu, in his well-known work *Etude médico-légale sur les attentats aux mœurs,* and Dr. Adolph note a peculiar infundibuliform disposition of the "after" and a smoothness and want of folds even before any abuse has taken place, together with special forms of the male organs in confirmed pederasts. But these observations have been rejected by Caspar, Hoffman, Brouardel and Dr. J. H. Henry Coutagne (*Notes sur la sodomie,* Lyon, 1880), and it is a medical question whose discussion would here be out of place.

The origin of pederasty is lost in the night of ages; but its historique has been carefully traced by many writers, especially Virey, Rosenbaum and M. H. E. Meir. The Ancient Greeks who, like the modern Germans, invented nothing but were great improvers of what other races invented, attributed the formal apostolate of Sotadism to Orpheus, whose stigmata were worn by the Thracian women;

Orpheus had rejected all love of women . . . . He was even the cause whereby the men of Thrace transferred their love to their own sex, toward boys in the brief springtime of life, whose first blossoms they plucked.

Ovid Met. x: 79-85.

Euripides proposed Laïus, father of Oedipus, as the inaugurator, whereas Timæus declared that the fashion of making favorites of boys was introduced into Greece from Crete, for Malthusian reasons said Aristotle, attributing it to Minos. Herodotus, however, knew far better, having discovered that the Orphic and Bacchic rites were originally Egyptian. But the father of history was a traveler and an annalist rather than an archaeologist and he tripped in the following passage:

"As soon as they (the Persians) hear of any luxury, they instantly make it their own, and hence, among other matters, they have learned from the Hellenes a passion for boys" ("unnatural lust" says modest Rawlinson). Plutarch asserts, with much more probability, that the Persians used eunuch boys according to the Greek fashion, long before they had seen the Grecian main.

In the Holy Books of the Hellenes, Homer and Hesiod, dealing with the heroic ages, there is no trace of pederasty, although, in a long subsequent generation, Lucian suspected Achilles and Patroclus as he did Orestes and Pylades, Theseus and Pirithous. Homer's praises of beauty are reserved for the feminines, especially his favorite, Helen. But the Dorians of Crete seem to have commended the abuse to Athens and Sparta and subsequently imported it into Tarentum, Agrigentum and other colonies. Ephorous in Strabo gives a curious account of the violent abduction of beloved boys by the lover; of the obligations of the ravisher to the favorite and of the "marriage-ceremonies" which lasted two months. Servius (Ad Æneid. x. 325) informs us; "We have it that the Cretans were overindulgent in their love of boys and that the habit later spread to Laconia and the whole of Greece." The Cretans and afterwards their apt pupils the Chalcidians held it disreputable for a beautiful boy to lack a lover. Hence Zeus the national Doric god of Crete loved Ganymede; Apollo, another Dorian deity, loved Hyacinth; and Hercules, a Doric hero who grew to be a sun god, loved Hylas and a host of others: thus Crete sanctified the practice by the examples of the gods and demigods. But when legislation came, the subject had qualified itself for legal limitation and as such was undertaken by Lycurgus and Solon, according to Xenophon, who draws a broad distinction between the honest love of boys and dishonest lust. They both approved of pure *pederastía,* like that of Harmodius and Aristogiton; but forbade it with serviles because degrading to a free man. Hence the love of boys was spoken of like that of women, e.g., "There was once a boy, or rather a youth, of exceeding beauty and he had many lovers'—this is the language of Hafiz and Sa'adi. Æschylus, Sophocles and Euripides were allowed to introduce it upon the stage, for "many men were as fond of having boys for their favorites as women for their mistresses; and this was a frequent fashion in many well-regulated cities of Greece." Poets like Alceus, Anacreon, Agathon and Pindar affected it and Theognis sang of a "beautiful boy in the flower of his youth." The statesmen Aristides and Themistocles quarreled over Stesileus of Teos; and Pisistratus loved Charmus, who first built an altar to Puerile Eros, while Charmus loved Hippias son of Pisistratus. Demosthenes, the orator, took into keeping a youth called Cnosion greatly to the indignation of his wife. Xenophon loved Clinias and Autolycus; Aristotle, Hermeas, Theodectes and others; Empedocles, Pausanias; Epicurus, Pytocles; Aristippus, Eutichydes and Zeno with his Stoics had a philosophic disregard for women, affecting only *pederastía.* A man in Atheneus left in his will that certain youths he had loved should fight like gladiators at his funeral; and Charicles in Lucian abuses Callicratidas for his love of "sterile pleasures." Lastly, there was the notable affair of Alcibiades and Socrates, the "saintly pederasts" being strongly suspected when under the mantle: "it was not often he rose unsullied from his side." Atheneus declares that Plato represents Socrates as absolutely intoxicated with his passion for Alcibiades. The ancients seem to have held the connection impure, or Juvenal would not have written

The foulest sewer of Socratic sodomy

followed by Firmicus who speaks of "Socratic buggery." It is the modern fashion to doubt the pederasty of the master of Hellenic Sophrosyne, the "Christian before Christianity"; but such a world-wide term as Socratic love can hardly be explained by the *lucus-a-non-lucendo* theory. We are overapt to apply our nineteenth-century prejudices and prepossessions to the morality of the ancient Greeks who would have specimened such squeamishness in Attic salt.

The Spartans, according to Agnon the Academic (confirmed by Plato, Plutarch and Cicero), treated boys and girls in the same way before marriage: hence Juvenal uses "Lacedemonius" for a pathic and other writers apply it to a tribate. After the Peloponnesian War, which ended in 404 B.C., the use became merged in the abuse. Yet some purity must have survived, even among the Bœotians who produced the famous Narcissus, described by Ovid:

Many young men and many girls desired him;
no young man nor any girl enjoyed him:

for Epaminondas, whose name is mentioned with three beloveds, established the Holy Regiment composed of mutual lovers, testifying the majesty of Eros and preferring to a discreditable life a glorious death. Philip's reflections on the fatal field of Chaeroneia form their fittest epitaph. At last the Athenians, according to Eschines, officially punished sodomy with death; but the threat did not abolish bordels of boys, like those of Karáchi; the Porneia and the Pornoboskeia, where slaves and boys for sale "stood," as the term was, near the Pnyx, the city walls and a certain tower, also about Lycabettus; and paid a fixed tax to the state. The pleasures of society in civilized Greece seem to have been sought chiefly in the heresies of love—Hetairesis and Sotadism.

It is calculated that the French of the sixteenth century had four hundred names for the parts genital and three hundred for their use in coition. The Greek vocabulary is not less copious and some of its pederastic terms, of which Meier gives nearly a hundred, and its nomenclature of pathologic love are curious and picturesque enough to merit quotation.

To live the life of Abron (the Argive) i.e., that of pathic or passive lover.

The Agathonian song.

Aischrourgía=dishonest love, also called Akolasía, Akrasía, Arrenokoitía, etc.

Alcinoan youths, or "non-conformists,"

> Juventus (Boy), taking more than fair care to
> save his skin.

Alegomenos, the "unspeakable," as the pederast was termed by the Council of Ancyra: also the Agrios, Apolaustus and Akolastos.

Androgyne, of whom Ausonius wrote:

> Lo, I am turned from boy to woman.

Badas and badízein=wriggling the buttocks: also Bátalosa= catamite.

Catapygos, Katapygosyne=lover of boys *and catadacty-*

lium from Dactylion, the ring, used in the sense of Nerissa's, but applied to the corollarium puerile.

Cinædus (Kínaidos), the active lover derived either from his kinetics or quasi=dog-modest. Also Spatalocinædus (*lasviciâ fluens*)=a fair Ganymede.

Chalcidissare (Khalkidizein), from Chalcis in Eubœa, a city famed for buttock love; mostly applied to licking the testicles by children.

Clazomenæ=the buttocks, also a sotadic disease, so called from the Ionian city devoted to Aversa Venus; also used of a pathic,

—and from behind the man is a woman.

Embasicœtas, prop. a link boy at marriages, also a "nightcap" drunk before bed and lastly an effeminate; one who wanders into anyone's bedroom (Catullus). See Encolpius' pun upon the Embasicete in Satyricon, chap. iv.

Epipedesis, the carnal assault.

Geiton lit. "neighbor" the beloved of Encolpius, which has produced the Fr. Giton=Bardache, Ital. bardascia from the Arab. Baradaj, a captive, a slave; the augm. form is Polygeiton.

Hippias (tyranny of) when the patient (woman or boy) mounts the agent. So also Kelitizein=*peccare superne or equum agitare supernum of* Horace.

Mokhthería, depravity with boys.

Paidika, whence pædicare (act) and pædicari (pass) = bugger: so in the Latin poet:

The beginning of PEnelope followed by the beginning of DIdo, and the start of CAnis, and the first syllable of Remis.

Pathikos, Pathicus, a passive, like Malakos malacus, mollis, facilis, Malchio, Trimalchio (Petronius), Malta, Maltha and in Hor. (Sat. ii. 25)

Malthinus strolls about with his clothes undone.

Praxis=the malpractice.

Pygisma=buttockry, because most actives end within the cheeks of the arse, being too much excited for further intromission.

Phœnicissare=cunnilinctus during the menstrual period, because this vice was particularly prevalent in Phœnicia (Thes. Erot. Ling. Latinæ); also *irrumer en miel*.

Phicidissare, signifies that act committed by dogs when they like the male or female genitals (Suetonius): also applied to pollution of childhood.

Samorium flores (Erasmus, Prov. xxiii.) alluding to the androgynic prostitutions of Samos.

Siphniassare (from Siphnos, *mod.* Sifanto Island)=to excite sexually by inserting the finger up the anus, says Erasmus (See Mirabau's Erotika Biblion, Anoscopie).

Thrypsis=the rubbing.

Pederastía had in Greece, I have shown, its noble and ideal side: Rome, however, borrowed her malpractices, like her religion and polity, from those ultramaterial Etruscans and debauched with a brazen face. Even under the Republic Plautus makes one of his characters exclaim, in the utmost sang-froid, "Push off, lover boy, get off my back!" With increased luxury the evil grew and Livy notices, at the Bacchanalia, more sex between man and man than between man and woman. There were individual protests; for instance, S. Q. Fabius Maximus Servilianus punished his son for a doubt of his chastity; and a private soldier, C. Plotius, killed his military Tribune, Q. Luscius, for unchaste proposals. The Lex Scantinia (Scatinia?), popularly derived from Scantinius the Tribune and of doubtful date (226 B.C.?), attempted to abate the scandal by fine and the Lex Julia by death; but they were trifling obstacles to the flood of infamy which surged in with the

Empire. No class seems then to have disdained these "sterile pleasures": in those days no mark of infamy attached to this form of love, as it has in Christian countries, says Bayle under "*Anacreon*." The great Cæsar, the "bald-headed bugger" of Catullus, was the husband of all the wives and the wife of all the husbands in Rome; and his soldiers sang in his praise "Caesar trod down Gaul, and Nicomedes trod Caesar" (Sueton lus. xlix.); whence his sobriquet "Bythinian tart." Of Augustus the people chanted

"Can't you see the Bugger has the world as his fingertip?"

Tiberius, with his "little fishes" and flocks of older boys, invented the Symplegma or nexus of Sellarii, active and passive, in which the *sprinthriæ* (lit. women's bracelets) were connected in a chain by the bond of flesh. Of this refinement, which in the earlier part of the nineteenth century was renewed by sundry Englishmen at Naples, Ausonius wrote:

Three in one bed and two of them being fucked;

And Martial had said:

Five coupled in a web of flesh; And in the chain are many held; etc.

Ausonius recounts of Caligula he so lost patience that he forcibly entered the priest M. Lepidus before the sacrifice was completed. The beautiful Nero was formally married to Pythagoras (or Doryphoros) and afterwards took to wife Sporus who was first subjected to castration of a peculiar fashion; he was then named Sabina after the deceased spouse and claimed queenly honors. The *"Otho-*

nis et Trajand pathici"* were famed; the great Hadrian openly loved Antinoüs and the wild debaucheries of Heliogabalus seem only to have amused, instead of disgusting, the Romans.

Uranopolis allowed public brothels where adults and *meritorii pueri*, who began their career as early as seven years, stood for hire: the inmates of these bordels wore sleeved tunics and dalmatics like women. As in modern Egypt pathic boys, we learn from Catullus, haunted the public baths. Debauchees had signals like freemasons whereby they recognized one another. The Greek Skematízein was made by closing the hand to represent the scrotum and raising the middle finger as if to feel whether a hen had eggs, *tâter si les poulettes ont l'œuf*: hence the Athenians called it Catapugon or sodomite and the Romans *digitus impudicus* or *infamis,** the "medical finger" of Rabelais and the Chiromantists. Another sign was to scratch the head with the minimus—*digitulo caput scabere.* The prostitution of boys was first forbidden by Domitian; but Saint Paul, a Greek, had formally expressed his abomination of *le vice*; and we may agree with Grotius that early Christianity did much to suppress it. At last the Emperor Theodosius punished it with fire as a profanation, because "the shrine of man's soul should be a holy-of-holies."

In the pagan days of imperial Rome her literature makes no difference between boy and girl. Horace naïvely says:

A young maidservant or a boy is at hand;

and with Hamlet, but in a dishonest sense:

*Otho's and Trojan's boys.
*The shameless or shameful finger.

40

—Man delights me not
Nor woman neither.

Similarly the Spaniard Martial, who is a mine of such pederastic allusions:

Whether a boy or girl smiles encouragement at you.

That marvelous Satyricon which unites the wit of Molière with the debaucheries of Piron, while the writer has been described, like Rabelais, as most pure in his impurity, is a kind of triumph of pederasty. Geiton the hero, a handsome curly-pated hobbledehoy of seventeen, with his flirtatious and wheedling tongue, is courted like any woman: his lovers are inordinately jealous of him and his desertion leaves deep scars upon the heart. But no dialogue between man and wife *in extremis* could be more pathetic than that in the scene where shipwreck is imminent. Elsewhere everyone seems to attempt his neighbor: a man with his tunic well tucked up assails Ascyltos; Lycus, the Tarentine skipper, would force Encolpius, and so forth: yet we have the neat and finished touch: "The lamentation was very fine (the dying man having manumitted his slaves) albeit his wife wept not as though she loved him. *How were it had he not behaved to her so well?"*

Erotic Latin glossaries give some ninety words connected with pederasty and some, which "speak with Roman simplicity," are peculiarly expressive. *"Aversa Venus"* alludes to women being treated as boys: hence Martial, translated by Piron, addresses Mistress Martial:

Think, then, dear wife, that you have two cunts.

The *capillatus* or *comatus** is also called *calamistratus,*

*Long-haired.

41

the darling curled with crisping-irons; and he is an *Effeminatus* i.e., one who plays the female role; or a *Delicatus,* slave or eunuch for the use of the Draucus (sodomite), Puerarius (boy lover) or Dominus (master). The divisor (divider) is so called from his practice of knocking or dividing the guts, something like Martial's filthy penis or Juvenal's running into yesterday's dinner. *Facere vicibus, incestare se invicem* or *mutuum facere* (to take it in turns, 80 at it turn and turn about, *or* do it together) is described as "a puerile vice," in which the two take turns to be active and passive: they are also called *Gemelli and Fratres***=compares in sodomy. *Illicita libido* (unlawful passion) is=sexual inversion, and is expressed by the picturesque phrase "to bend someone over." *Depilatus, divellere pilos, glaber, lœvis and nates pervellere* (plucked, pull out the hair, bald, smooth *and* bald-arsed) are allusions to the Sotadic toilette. The fine distinction between *demittere and dejicere caput* are worthy of a glossary, while *Pathica puella* (pathic girl) *puera* (girl-boy) *putus* (boy) *pullipremo* (boy-squeezer) *pusio* (dormouse) *pygiaca sacra* (the sacred rites of the arse-hole) *quadrupes* (four-footed beast) *scarabœus* (beetle) and *smerdalius* (a terrible epithet applied to the Priapic phallus) explain themselves.

From Rome the practice extended far and wide to her colonies, especially the Provincia now called Provence. Athenæus charges the people of Massilia with "acting like women out of luxury"; and he cites the saying "May you sail to Massilia!" as if it were another Corinth. Indeed the whole Celtic race is charged with *le vice* by Aristotle and Diodorus Siculus. Roman civilization carried pederasty also to northern Africa, where it took firm root, while the Negro and Negroid races to the South ignore the erotic

**Twins and Brothers.

perversion, except where imported by foreigners into such kingdoms as Bornu and Haussa. In old Mauritania, now Morocco, the Moors proper are notable sodomites; Moslems, even of saintly houses, are permitted openly to keep catamites, nor do their disciples think worse of their sanctity for such license: in one case the English wife failed to banish from the home "that horrid boy."

Yet pederasty is forbidden by the Koran. In chapter iv, 20 we read: "And if two (men) among you commit the crime, then punish them both," the penalty being some hurt or damage by public reproach, insult or scourging. There are four distinct references to Lot and the Sodomites in chapters vii, 78; xi 77-84; xvi 160-174 and xixx 28-35. In the first the prophet commissioned to the people says, "Proceed ye to fullsome act wherein no creature hath forgone ye? Verily ye come to men in lieu of women lustfully." We have then an account of the rain which Gabriel, seeing the distress of his host, smote them on the Cities of the Plain is repeated with more detail in the second reference. Here the angels, generally supposed to be three, Gabriel, Michael and Raphael, appeared to Lot as beautiful youths, a sore temptation to the sinners and the godly man's arm was straitened concerning his visitors because he felt unable to protect them from the erotic vagaries of his fellow townsmen. Therefore, he shut his doors and from behind them argued the matter: presently the riotous assembly attempted to climb the wall when Gabriel, seeing the distress of his host, smote them on the face with one of his wings and blinded them so that all moved off crying for aid and saying that Lot had magicians in his house. Hereupon the "cities" which, if they ever existed, must have been Fellah villages, were uplifted: Gabriel thrust his wing under them and raised them so high that the inhabitants of the lower heaven (the lunar sphere) could hear the dogs barking and the cocks crowing. Then came the rain of stones: these were clay pellets baked in hellfire, streaked white and red, or having some mark to distinguish them from the ordinary and each bearing the name of its destination like the missiles which destroyed the host of Abrahat al-Ashram. Lastly the "cities" were turned upside down and cast upon earth. These circumstantial unfacts are repeated at full length in the other two chapters; but rather as an instance of Allah's power than as a warning against pederasty, which Mohammed seems to have regarded with philosophic indifference. The general opinion of his followers was that it should be punished like fornication unless the offenders made a public act of penitence. But here, as in adultery, the law is somewhat too clement and will not convict unless four credible witnesses swear to have seen the thing actually happening. I have noticed the vicious opinion that the Ghilmán or Wuldán, the beautiful boys of Paradise, the counterparts of the Houris, will be lawful catamites to the True Believers in a future state of happiness: the idea is nowhere countenanced in Al-Islam; and, although I have often heard debauchees refer to it, the learned look upon the assertion is scandalous.

As in Morocco so the vice prevails throughout the old regencies of Algiers, Tunis and Tripoli and all the cities of the South Mediterranean seaboard, while it is unknown to the Nubians, the Berbers and the wilder tribes dwelling inland. Proceeding eastward we reach Egypt, that classical region of all abominations which, marvelous to relate, flourished in closest contact with men leading the purest of lives, models of moderation and morality, of religion and virtue. Among the ancient Copts *le vice* was part and portion of the ritual and was represented by two male partridges alternately copulating. The evil would have gained strength by the invasion of Cambyses (524 B.C.), whose armies, after the victory over Psammenitus, settled in the

Nile Valley and held it, despite sundry revolts, for some hundred and ninety years. During these six generations the Iranians left their mark upon Lower Egypt and especially, as the late Rogers Bey proved, upon the Fayyum the most ancient Delta of the Nile. Nor would the evil be diminished by the Hellenes who, under Alexander the Great, "liberator and savior of Egypt" (322 B.C.), extinguished the native dynasties: the love of the Macedonian for Bagoas the Eunuch being a matter of history. From that time and under the rule of the Ptolemies the morality gradually decayed; the Canopic orgies extended into private life the debauchery of the men was equaled only by the depravity of the women. Neither Christianity nor Al-Islam could effect a change for the better; and social morality seems to have been at its worst during the past century when Sonnini traveled (A.D. 1717). The French officer, who is thoroughly trustworthy, draws the darkest picture of the widely spread criminality, especially of the bestiality and the sodomy which formed the "delight of the Egyptians." During the Napoleonic conquest Jaubert in his letter to General Bruix says, "The Arabs and the Mamelukes treated some of the prisoners in the same way as Socrates is supposed to have treated Alcibiades. It was dishonor or death." Old Anglo-Egyptians still chuckle over the tale of St'id Pasha and M. de Ruyssenaer, the high-dried and highly respectable Consul-General for the Netherlands, who was solemnly advised to make the experiment, active and passive, before offering his opinion upon the subject.

In the present age extensive intercourse with Europeans has produced not a reformation but a certain reticence among the upper classes: they are as vicious as ever, but they do not care for displaying their vices to the eyes of mocking strangers.

Syria and Palestine, another ancient focus of abominations, borrowed from Egypt and exaggerated the worship of Androgynic and hermaphroditic deities. Plutarch notes that the old Nilotes held the moon to be of "male-female sex," the men sacrificing to Luna and the women to Lunus. Isis also was a hermaphrodite, the idea being that Æther or Air (the lower heavens) was the menstruum of generative nature; and Damascius explained the tenet by the all-fruitful and prolific powers of the atmosphere. Hence the fragment attributed to Orpheus, the song of Jupiter:

All things from Jove descend
Jove was a male, Jove was a deathless bride;
For men call Air, of two-fold sex, the Jove.

Julius Firmicus relates that "the Assyrians and part of the Africans" (along the Mediterranean seaboard?) "hold Air to be the chief element and adore its fanciful figure (*imaginata figura*), consecrated under the name of Juno or the Virgin Venus. . . . Their companies of priests cannot duly serve her unless they effeminate their faces, smooth their skins and disgrace their masculine sex by feminine ornaments. You may see men in their very temples amid general groans enduring miserable dalliance and becoming passives like women (*viros muliebria pati*) and they expose, with boasting and ostentation, the pollution of the impure and immodest body." Here we find the religious significance of eunuchry. It was practised as a religious rite by the Tympanotribas or Gallus, the castrated votary of Rhea or Bona Mater, in Phrygia called Cybele, self-mutilated but not in memory of Atys; and by a host of other creeds; even Christianity, as sundry texts show, could not altogether cast out the old possession. Here too we have an explanation of Sotadic love in its second stage, when it became, like cannibalism, a matter of superstition.

46

Assuming a nature-implanted tendency, we see that like human sacrifice it was held to be the most acceptable offering to the god-goddesses in the Orgia or sacred ceremonies, a something set apart for peculiar worship. Hence in Rome as in Egypt the temples of Isis (*Inachidos limina, Isiacæ sacraria Lunæ*) were centers of sodomy and the religious practice was adopted by the grand priestly castes from Mesopotamia to Mexico and Peru.

We find the earliest written notices of the vice in the mythical destruction of the Pentapolis, Sodom, Gomorrah (= 'Amirah, the cultivated country), Adama, Zeboïm and Zoar or Bela. The legend has been amply embroidered by the rabbis who make the Sodomites do everything backwards: e.g., if a man were wounded he was fined for bloodshed and was compelled to pay the offender; and if one cut off the ear of a neighbor's ass he was condemned to keep the animal till the ear grew again.

The Jewish doctors declare the people to have been a race of sharpers with rogues for magistrates, and thus they justify the judgment which they read literally. But the traveler cannot accept it. I have carefully examined the lands at the north and at the south of that most beautiful lake, the so-called Dead Sea, whose tranquil loveliness, backed by the grand plateau of Moab, is an object of admiration to all save patients suffering from the strange disease "Holy Land on the Brain." But I found no trace of craters in the neighborhood, no signs of vulcanism, no remains of "meteoric stones": the asphalt which named the water is a mineralized vegetable washed out of the limestones, and the sulphur and salt are brought down by the Jordan into a lake without issue. I must therefore look upon the history as a myth which may have served a double purpose. The first would be to deter the Jew from the Malthusian practices of his pagan predecessors, upon which obloquy was cast, so far resembling the scandalous

47

and absurd legend which explained the names of the children of Lot by Pheiné and Thamma as "Moab" (Mu-ab) the water or semen of the father, and "Ammon" as mother's son, that is, bastard. The fable would also account for the abnormal fissure containing the lower Jordan and the Dead Sea, which the late Sir R. I. Murchison used wrong-headedly to call a "Volcano of Depression": this geological feature, that cuts off the river basin from its natural outlet the Gulf of Eloth (Akabah), must date from myriad years before there were "Cities of the Plains." But the main object of the ancient lawgiver, Osariph, Moses or the Moseidæ, was doubtless to discountenance a perversion prejudicial to the increase of population. And he speaks with no uncertain voice, "Whoso lieth with a beast shall surely be put to death. If a man lie with mankind as he lieth with a woman, both of them have committed an abomination: they shall surely be put to death; their blood shall be upon them." Again, "there shall be no whore of the daughters of Israel nor a sodomite of the sons of Israel."

The old commentators on the Sodom-myth are most unsatisfactory, e.g., Parkhurst, Kadesh. "From hence we may observe the peculiar propriety of this punishment of Sodom and of the neighboring cities. By their sodomitical impurities they meant to acknowledge the Heavens as the cause of fruitfulness independently upon, and in opposition to, Jehovah; therefore Jehovah, by raining upon them not genial showers but brimstone from heaven, not only destroyed the inhabitants but also changed all that country, which was before as the garden of God, into brimstone and salt that is not sown nor beareth, neither any grass groweth therein."

It must be owned that to this Pentapolis was dealt very hard measure for religiously and diligently practicing a popular rite which a host of cities even in the present day, as Naples and Shiraz, to mention no others, affect for simple luxury and affect with impunity. The myth may probably reduce itself to very small proportions, a few Fellah villages destroyed by a storm, like that which drove Brennus from Delphi.

The Hebrews entering Syria found it religionized by Assyria and Babylonia, whence Accadian Ishtar had passed west and had become Ashtoreth, Ashtaroth or Ashirab, the Anaitis of Armenia, the Phœnician Astarte and the Greek Aphrodite, the great Moon-goddess, who is queen of Heaven and Love. In another phase she was Venus Mylitta=the Procreatrix, in Chaldaic Mauludatá and in Arabic Moawallidah, she who bringeth forth. She was worshiped by men habited as women and vice versa; for which reason in the Torah the sexes are forbidden to change dress. The male prostitutes were called Kadesh the holy, the women being Kadeshah, and doubtless gave themselves up to great excesses. Eusebius describes a school of impurity at Aphac, where women and "men who were not men" practiced all manner of abominations in honor of the Demon (Venus). Here the Phrygian symbolism of Kybele and Attis (Atys) had become the Syrian Ba'al Tammuz and Astarte, and the Grecian Dioniæ and Adonis, the anthropomorphic forms of the two greater lights. The site, Apheca, now Wady al-Afik on the route from Bayrut to the Cedars, is a glen of wild and wondrous beauty, fitting framework for the loves of goddess and demigod: and the ruins of the temple destroyed by Constantine contrast with Nature's work, the glorious fountain, more glittering than glass, which feeds the River Ibrahim and still at times Adonis runs purple to the sea.

The Phœnicians spread this androgynic worship over Greece. We find the consecrated servants and votaries of Corinthian Aphrodite called Hierodouli, who aided the ten thousand courtesans in gracing the Venus temple: from this excessive luxury arose the proverb popularized by Horace. One of the headquarters of the cult was Cyprus where, as Servius relates, stood the simulacre of a bearded Aphrodite with feminine body and costume, sceptered and mitered like a man. The sexes, when worshiping it, exchanged habits and here the virginity was offered in sacrifice: Herodotus describes this defloration at Babylon but sees only the shameful part of the custom which was a mere consecration of a tribal rite. Everywhere, girls before marriage belong either to the father or to the clan and thus the maiden paid the debt due to the public before becoming private property as a wife. The same usage prevailed in ancient Armenia and in parts of Ethiopia; and Herodotus tells us that a practice very much like the Babylonian "is found also in certain parts of the Island of Cyprus": it is noticed by Justin and probably it explains the "Succoth Benoth" or Damsels' booths which the Babylonians transplanted to the cities of Samaria. The Jews seem very successfully to have copied the abominations of their pagan neighbors, even in the matter of the "dog." In the reign of wicked Rehoboam (975 B.C.) "There were also sodomites in the land and they did according to all the abominations of the nations which the Lord cast out before the children of Israel." The scandal was abated by zealous King Asa (958 B.C.) whose grandmother was high-priestess of Priapus (princeps in sacris Priapi): he "took away the sodomites out of the land." Yet the prophets were loud in their complaints, especially the so called Isaiah, "except the Lord of Hosts had left to us a very small remnant, we should have been as Sodom"; and strong measures were required from good King Josiah (641 B.C.) who amongst other things, "brake down the houses of the sodomites that were by the house of the Lord, where the women wove hangings for the grove."

The bordels of boys ("they clove unto strange boys") appear to have been near the Temple.

Syria has not forgotten her old "praxis." At Damascus, I found some noteworthy cases among the religious of the great Amawl Mosque. As for the Druses we have Burckhardt's authority: "unnatural propensities are very common among them."

The Sotadic Zone covers the whole of Asia Minor and Mesopotamia now occupied by the "unspeakable Turk," a race of born pederasts; and in the former region we first notice a peculiarity of the feminine figure, the drooping, flat and baggy breast, which prevails over all this part of the belt. While the women to the north and south have, with local exceptions, the upright breasts of the European virgin,* those of Turkey, Persia, Afghanistan and Kashmir lose all the fine curves of the bosom, sometimes even before the first child; and after it the hemispheres take the form of bags. This cannot result from climate only; the women of Marathá-land, inhabiting a damper and hotter region than Kashmir, are noted for fine firm breasts even after parturition. *Le vice* of course prevails more in the cities and towns of Asiatic Turkey than in the villages; yet even these are infected; while the nomad Turcomans contrast badly in this point with the gypsies, those Bedouin of India. The Kurd population is of Iranian origin, which means that the evil is deeply rooted: I have noted in *The Nights* that the great and glorious Saladin was a habitual pederast. The Armenians, as their national character is, will prostitute themselves for gain but prefer women to boys: Georgia supplied Turkey with catamites, while Circassia sent concubines. In Mesopotamia, the barbarous invader has almost obliterated the ancient

---

* A noted exception is Vienna, remarkable for the enormous development of the virginal bosom and soon becomes pendant.

51

civilization which is antedated only by the Nilotic; the mysteries of old Babylon nowhere survive save in certain obscure tribes like the Mandæans, the Devil-worshipers and the Alí-iláhi. Entering Persia we find the reverse of Armenia; and, despite Herodotus, I believe that Iran borrowed her pathologic love from the peoples of the Tigris-Euphrates Valley and not from the then insignificant Greeks. But whatever may be its origin, the corruption is now bred in the bone. It begins in boyhood and many Persians account for it by paternal severity. Youths arriving at puberty found none of the facilities with which Europe supplies fornication. Onanism is, to a certain extent, discouraged by circumcision, and meddling with the father's slave girls and concubines would be risking cruel punishment, if not death. Hence, they use each other by turns, a "puerile practice" known as Alish-Takish, the Latin *facere vicibus* (taking turns) or *mutuum facere* (turn and turn about). Temperament, media, and atavism recommend the custom to the general; and after marrying and begetting heirs, Paterfamilias returns to the Ganymede. Hence all the odes of Hafiz are addressed to youth, as proved by such Arabic exclamations as "*Afaka'llah*=Allah assail thee (masculine)": the object is often fanciful but it would be held coarse and immodest to address an imaginary girl. An illustration of the penchant is told at Shiraz concerning a certain Mujtahid, the head of the Shilah creed, corresponding with a prince-archbishop in Europe. A friend once said to him:

"There is a question I would fain address to your Eminence but I lack the daring to do so." "Ask and fear not," replied the Divine. "It is this, O Mujtahid! Figure thee in a garden of roses and hyacinths with the evening breeze waving the cypress heads, a fair youth of twenty sitting by thy side and the assurance of perfect privacy. What, prithee, would be the result?" The holy man bowed the chin of doubt upon the collar of meditation; and, too honest to lie, presently whispered, "Allah defend me from such temptation of Satan!"

Yet even in Persia men have not been wanting who have done their utmost to uproot the vice: in the same Shiraz they speak of a father who, finding his son in flagrant delict, put him to death like Brutus or Lynch of Galway. However, such isolated cases can effect nothing. Chardin tells us that houses of male prostitution were common in Persia while those of women were unknown: the same is the case in the present day, and the boys are prepared with extreme care by diet, baths, depilation, unguents and a host of artists in cosmetics. *Le vice* is looked upon at most as a peccadillo and its mention crops up in every jest book. When the Isfahan man mocked Shaykh Sa'adi by comparing the bald pates of Shirazian elders to the bottom of a lotá, a brass cup with a wide-necked opening used in the Hammam, the witty poet turned its aperture upwards and thereto likened the well-abused podex of an Isfahani youth. Another favorite piece of Shirazian "chaff" is to declare that when an Isfahan father would set up his son in business he provides him with a pound of rice, meaning that he can sell the result as compost for the kitchen garden, and with the price buy another meal: hence the saying *Khakh-i-pái-káhú*=the soil at the lettuce root. The Isfahanis retort with the name of a station or halting place between the two cities where, under pretense of making travelers stow away their riding gear, many a Shirári had been raped: hence *"Zin o takaltú tú bi-bar'*=carry within saddle and saddlecloth! A favorite Persian punishment for strangers caught in the Harem or Gynæceum is to strip and throw them and expose them to the embraces of the grooms and Negro slaves. I once asked a Shirazi how penetration was possible if the patient resisted with all the force of the sphincter muscle: he smiled and said, "Ah, we Persians know a trick to get over that; we apply a sharpened tent peg to the crupper bone (os coccygis) and knock till he opens." A well-known missionary to the East during the last generation was subjected to this gross insult by one of the Persian prince-governors, whom he had infuriated by his conversion mania: in his memoirs he alludes to it by mentioning his "dishonored person"; but English readers cannot comprehend the full significance of the confession. About the same time, Shaykh Nasr, Governor of Bushire, a man gamed for facetious blackguardism, used to invite European youngsters serving in the Bombay Marine and ply them with liquor till they were insensible. Next morning the middies mostly complained that the champagne had caused a curious irritation and soreness in *la parte-poste*. The same Eastern "Scrogin" would ask his guests if they had ever seen a man-cannon (Adami-top); and, on their replying in the negative, a gray-beard slave was dragged in blaspheming and struggling with all his strength. He was presently placed on all fours and firmly held by the extremities; his bag-trousers were let down and a dozen peppercorns were inserted up his anus: the target was a sheet of paper held at a reasonable distance; the match was applied by a pinch of cayenne in the victim's nostrils; the sneeze started the grapeshot and the number of hits on the butt decided the bets. We can hardly wonder at the loose conduct of Persian women perpetually mortified by marital pederasty. During the unhappy campaign of 1856-57 in which, with the exception of a few brilliant skirmishes, we gained no glory, Sir James Outram and the Bombay Army showing how badly they could work, there was a formal outburst of the harems; and even women of princely birth could not be kept out of the officers' quarters.

54

The cities of Afghanistan and Sind are thoroughly saturated with Persian vice, and the people sing

Kadr-i-kus Aughán dánad, kadr-i-kunrá Kábuli:
The worth of coynte the Afghan knows: Cabul
prefers the other chose!

The Afghans are commercial travelers on a large scale and each caravan is accompanied by a number of boys and lads almost in woman's attire with kohled eyes and rouged cheeks, long tresses and hennaed fingers and toes, riding luxuriously in Kajáwas or camel-panniers: they are called Kúchi-safari, or traveling wives, and the husbands trudge patiently by their sides. In Afghanistan also a frantic debauchery broke out among the women when they found incubi who were not pederasts; and the scandal was not the most insignificant cause of the general rising at Cabul (November 1841), and the slaughter of Macnaghten, Burnes and other British officers.

Resuming our way eastward we find the Sikhs and the Moslems of the Panjab much addicted to *le vice,* although the Himalayan tribes to the north and those lying south, the Rájputs and Marathás, ignore it. The same may be said of the Kashmirians, who add another Kappa to the triad Kakista, Kappadocians, Kretans, and Kilicians: the proverb says,

Agar kaht-i-mardum uftad, az ín sih jins kam gírí;
Eki Afghán, dovvuin Sindi, siyyum badjinsi-i-Kashmírí:

Though of men there be famine yet shun these three—
Afghan, Sindi and rascally Kashmírí.

M. Louis Daville describes the infamies of Lahore and Lakhnau where he found men dressed as women, with flowing locks under crowns of flowers, imitating the feminine walk and gestures, voice and fashion of speech, and ogling their admirers with all the coquetry of bayaderes.

Victor Jacquemont's *Journal de Voyage* describes the pederasty of Ranjít Singh, the "Lion of the Panjáb," and has pathic Guláb Singh whom the English inflicted upon Cashmir as ruler by way of paying for his treason. Yet the Hindus, I repeat, hold pederasty in abhorrence and are as much scandalized by being called *Gánd-márá* (anus beater) or *Gándú* (anuser) as Englishmen would be. During the years 1843-44, my regiment, almost all Hindu Sepoys of the Bombay Presidency, was stationed at a purgatory called Bandar Chárrá, a sandy flat with a scatter of verdigris-green milk-bush some forty miles north of Karachi the headquarters. The dirty heap of mud and mat hovels, which represented the adjacent native village, could not supply a single woman: yet only one case of pederasty came to light and that after a tragic fashion some years afterwards. A young Brahman had connection with a soldier comrade of low caste and this had continued till, in an unhappy hour, the Pariah patient ventured to become the agent. The latter, in Arab, *Al-Fá'il* the "doer," is not an object of contempt like Al-Mafúl the "done"; and the high-caste Sepoy, stung by remorse and revenge, loaded his musket and deliberately shot his paramour. He was hanged by court-martial at Hyderabad and, when his last wishes were asked, he begged in vain to be suspended by the feet; the idea being that his soul, polluted by exiting "below the waist," would be doomed to endless transmigrations through the lowest forms of life.

Beyond India, I have stated, the Sotadic Zone begins to broaden out embracing all China, Turkistan and Japan. The Chinese, as far as we know them in the great cities, are omnivorous and *omnifutuentes*: they are the chosen people of debauchery and their systematic bestiality with ducks, goats, and other animals is equaled only by their pederasty. Kæmpfer and Orlof Torée (*Voyage en Chine*) notice the public houses for boys and youths in China and Japan. Mirabeau (*L'Anandryne*) describes the tribadism of their women in hammocks. When Pekin was plundered the harems contained a number of balls a little larger than the old musket-bullet, made of thin silver with a loose pellet of brass inside somewhat like a grelot: these articles were placed by the women between the labia and an up-and-down movement on the bed gave a pleasant titillation when nothing better was to be procured. They have every artifice of luxury, aphrodisiacs, erotic perfumes and singular applications. Such are the pills which, dissolved in water and applied to the glans penis, cause it to throb and swell: so, according to Amerigo Vespucci, American women could artificially increase the size of their husbands' parts. The Chinese bracelet of caoutchouc studded with points now takes the place of the Herisson, or ring of hair, which was bound between the glans and prepuce. Of the artificial penis, that imitation of the Tree of Life or Soter Kosmou, which the Latins called *phallus* and *fascinum,* the French *godemiché* and the Italians *passatempo* and *diletto* (whence our *"dildo"*), every kind abounds, varying from a stuffed "French letter" to a cone of ribbed horn which looks like an instrument of torture. For the use of men they have the "merkin," a heart-shaped article of thin skin stuffed with cotton and slit with an artificial vagina: two tapes at the top and one below lash it to the back of a chair. The erotic literature of the Chinese and Japanese is highly developed and their illustrations are often facetious, as well as obscene. All are familiar with that of the strong man who by a blow with his enormous phallus shivers a copper pot; and the ludicrous contrast of the hugh-membered wights who land in the Isle of Women and presently escape from it, wrinkled and shriveled, true Domine Dolittles. Of Turkistan we know little, but what we know confirms my statement. Mr. Schuyler in his *Turkistan* offers an illustration of a "Batcah" (Pers. *bachcheh*=catamite), "or singing-boy surrounded by his admirers." Of the Tartars Master Purchas laconically says, "They are addicted to Sodomie or Buggerie." The learned casuist, Thomas Sanchez, the Spaniard had (says Mirabeau in Kadhésh) to decide a difficult question concerning the sinfulness of a peculiar erotic perversion. The Jesuits brought home from Manila a tailed man whose movable prolongation of the os coccygis measured from 7 to 10 inches: he had placed himself between two women, enjoying one naturally while the other used his tail as an artificial penis. The verdict was incomplete sodomy and simple fornication. For the islands north of Japan, the "Sodomitical Sea," and the "nayle of tynne" thrust through the prepuce to prevent sodomy.

Passing over to America, we find that the Sotadic Zone contains the whole hemisphere from Behring's Strait to Magellan's Strait. This prevalence of "mollities" astonishes the anthropologist, who is apt to consider pederasty the growth of luxury and the especial product of great and civilized cities, unnecessary and therefore unknown to simple savagery where the births of both sexes are about equal and female infanticide is not practiced. In many parts of the New World, this perversion was accompanied by another depravity of taste, confirmed cannibalism. The forests and campos abounded in game from the deer to the pheasantlike penelope, and the seas and rivers produced an unfailing supply of excellent fish and shellfish; yet the Brazilian Tupis preferred the meat of man to every other food.

A glance at Mr. Bancroft proves the abnormal development of sodomy among the savages and barbarians of the New World. Even his half-frozen Hyperboreans "possess all the passions which are supposed to develop most freely under a milder temperature." The voluptuousness and polygamy of the North American Indians, under a temperature of almost perpetual winter, is far greater than that of the most sensual tropical nations. I can quote only a few of the most remarkable instances. Of the Koniagas of Kadiak Island and the Thinkleets we read, "The most repugnant of all their practices is that of male concubinage. A Kadiak mother will select her handsomest and most promising boy, and dress and rear him as a girl, teaching him only domestic duties, keeping him at women's work, associating him with women and girls, in order to render his effeminacy complete. Arriving at the age of ten or fifteen years, he is married to some wealthy man who regards such a companion as a great acquisition. These male concubines are called *Achnutschik* or *Schopans"* (the authorities quoted being Holmberg, Langsdorff, Billing, Choris, Lisiansky and Marchand). The same is the case in Nutka Sound and the Aleutian Islands, where "male concubinage obtains throughout, but not to the same extent as amongst the Koniagas." The objects of "unnatural" affection have their beards carefully plucked out as soon as the face-hair begins to grow, and their chins are tattooed like those of the women. In California, the first missionaries found the same practice, the youths being called Joya (Bancroft, and authorities Palon, Crespi, Boscana, Mofras, Torquemada, Duflot and Fages). The Comanches unite incest with sodomy.

"In New Mexico according to Arlegui, Ribas, and other authors, male concubinage prevails to a great extent, these loathsome semblances of humanity, whom to call beastly were a slander upon beasts, dress themselves in the clothes and perform the functions of women, the use of weapons being denied them." Pederasty was systematically practiced by the peoples of Cuba, Careta, and other parts of Central America. The Caciques and some of the headmen kept harems of youths who, as soon as destined for the unclean office, were dressed as women. They went by the name of Camayoas, and were hated and detested by the goodwives. Of the Nahua nations Father Pierre de Gand (alias Oe Musa) writes, "A certain number of priests had no wives at all, but in their place boys whom they used obscenely. The sin was so common to the country, that all, young and old alike, were infected by it. It had such a hold upon them, that even boys of six were addicted to it." Among the Mayas of Yucatan, Las Casas declares that the great prevalence of "unnatural" lust made parents anxious to see their progeny wedded as soon as possible. In Vera Paz a god, called by some Chin and by others Cavial and Maran, taught it by committing the act with another god. Some fathers gave their sons a boy to use as a woman, and if any other approached this pathic he was treated as an adulterer. In Yucatan, images were found by Bernal Diaz proving the sodomitical propensities of the people. De Pauw has much to say about the subject in Mexico generally: in the northern provinces men married youths who, dressed like women, were forbidden to carry arms. According to Gomara, there were at Tamalipas houses of male prostitution; and from Diaz and others we gather that the beastly sin was the rule. Both in Mexico and in Peru it might have caused, if it did not justify, the cruelties of the Conquistadores. Pederasty was also general throughout Nicaragua, and the early explorers found it among the indigenes of Panama.

We have authentic details concerning *le vice* in Peru and its adjacent lands, beginning with Cieza de Leon, who must be read in the original or in the translated extracts of Purchas, not in the cruelly castrated form preferred by the Council of the Hakluyt Society. Speaking of the New Granada Indians he tells us that "at Old Port (Porto Viejo) and Puna, the *Deuill so farre prevayled in their beastly Deuotions that there were Boyes consecrated to serue in the Temple; and at the times of their Sacrifices and Solemme Feasts, the Lords and principall men abused them to that detestable filthinesse";* i.e. performed their peculiar worship.

Generally in the hill countries the Devil, under the show of holiness, had introduced the practice, for every temple or chief house of adoration kept one or two men or more who were attired like women, even from the time of their childhood, and spoke like them, imitating them in everything; with these, under pretext of holiness and religion, their principal men on principal days had commerce. Speaking of the arrival of the Giants at Point Santa Elena, Cieza says, they were detested by the natives, because in using their women they killed them and their men also in another way. All the natives declare that God brought upon them a punishment proportioned to the enormity of their offense. When they were engaged together in their accursed intercourse, a fearful and terrible fire came down from Heaven with a great noise, out of the midst of which there issued a shining angel with a glittering sword, wherewith at one blow they were all killed and the fire consumed them. There remained a few bones and skulls which God allowed to bide unconsumed by the fire, as a memorial of this punishment. In the Hakluyt Society's bowdlerization, we read of the Tumbez Islanders being "very vicious, many of them committing the abominable offense"; also, "If by the advice of the Devil any Indian commit the abominable crime, it is thought little of

61

and they call him a woman." In chapters 52 and 53 we find exceptions. The Indians of Huancabamba, "although so near the peoples of Puerto Viejo and Guayaquil, do not commit the abominable sin"; and the Serranos, or island mountaineers, as sorcerers and magicians inferior to the coast peoples, were not so much addicted to sodomy.

The Royal Commentaries of the Incas shows that the evil was of a comparatively modern growth. In the early period of Peruvian history, the people considered the crime "unspeakable": if a Cuzco Indian, not of Incarial blood, angrily addressed the term pederast to another, he was held infamous for many days. One of the generals having reported to the Inca Ccapacc Yuqanqui that there were some sodomites, not in all the valleys but one here and one there, "nor was it a habit of all the inhabitants but only of certain persons who practiced it privately"; the ruler ordered that the criminals should be publicly burned alive and their houses, crops and trees destroyed: moreover, to show his abomination, he commanded that the whole village should so be treated if one man fell into this habit. Elsewhere we learn:

"There were sodomites in some provinces, though not openly nor universally, but some particular men and in secret. In some parts, they had them in their temples, because the Devil persuaded them that the gods took great delight in such people, and thus the Devil acted as a traitor to remove the veil of shame that the Gentiles felt for this crime and to accustom them to commit it in public and in common."

During the times of the Conquistadores, male concubinage had become the rule throughout Peru. At Cuzco, we are told by Nuno de Guzman in 1530:

The last which was taken, and which fought most cou-

ragiously, was a man in the habite of a woman, which confessed that from a childe he had gotten his liuing by that filthinesse, for which I caused him to be burned.

V. F. Lopez draws a frightful picture of pathologic love in Peru. Under the reigns which followed that of Inti-Kapak (Ccapacc) Amauri, the country was attacked by invaders of a giant race coming from the sea: they practiced pederasty after a fashion so shameless that the conquered tribes were compelled to fly. Under the pre-Incarial Amauta, or priestly dynasty, Peru had lapsed into savagery and the kings of Cuzco preserved only the name. "All this shame and misery stemmed from the two unspeakable vices—sodomy and bestiality. The women were particularly outraged to see the laws of Nature thus offended. Whenever they met, they would bitterly complain of their wretched lot and of the contemptuous way in which they were treated. . . . The world was turned upside-down, man loved man and suffered jealousy of his own sex. . . The women sought in vain to alleviate their sorry state. They used philters and black magic. This brought a few individuals back, but could not stop the ceaseless spread of the vice. This state of affairs created a real Dark Age, which lasted until the rule of the Incas."

When Sinchi Roko (the nineteenth of Montesinos and the twentieth of Garcilazo) became Inca, he found morals at the lowest ebb. "Neither the wisdom of the Inca nor the severe laws which he had pronounced could entirely root out this unnatural vice. It broke out again with renewed vigor, and women grew so jealous that very many of them murdered their husbands as a result. Seers and sorcerers spent all their days compounding, with certain drugs, magic philters which sent those who ate them mad, and these the women gave to those of whom they were jealous, either in their food or in their *chicha*."

I have remarked that the Tupi races of Brazil were infamous for cannibalism and sodomy; nor could the latter be only racial as proved by the fact that colonists of pure Lusitanian blood followed in the path of the savages. Sr. Antonio Augusto da Costa Aguiar is outspoken upon this point. "A crime which in England leads to the gallows, and which is the very measure of abject depravity, passes with impunity amongst us by the participating in it of almost all or of many (*de quasi todos, ou de muitos*). Ah! if the wrath of Heaven were to fall by the way of punishing such crimes (*delictos*) more than one city of this Empire, more than a dozen, would pass into the category of the Sodoms and Gomorrahs." Till late years pederasty in Brazil was looked upon as a peccadillo; the European immigrants following the practice of the wild men who were naked but not, as Columbus said, "clothed in innocence." One of Her Majesty's consuls used to tell a tale of the hilarity provoked in a "fashionable" assembly by the open declaration of a young gentleman that his mulatto "patient" had suddenly turned upon him, insisting upon becoming agent. Now, however, under the influences of improved education and respect for the public opinion of Europe, pathologic love among the Luso-Brazilians has been reduced to the normal limits.

Outside the Sotadic Zone, I have said, *le vice* is sporadic, not endemic: yet the physical and moral effect of great cities where puberty, they say, is induced earlier than in country sites, has been the same in most lands, causing modesty to decay and pederasty to flourish. The Badawi Arab is wholly pure of *le vice*; yet San'á the capital of Al-Yaman and other centers of population have long been and still are thoroughly infected. History tells us of Zú

64

Shanátir, tyrant of "Arabia Felix," in A.D. 478, who used to entice young men into his palace and cause them after use to be cast out of the windows: this unkindly ruler was at last poinarded by the youth Zerash, known from his long ringlets as "Zú Nowás." The Negro race is mostly untainted by sodomy and tribadism. Yet Joan dos Sanctos found in Cacango of West Africa certain *"Chibudi, which are men attyred like women and behaue themselves womanly, ashamed to be called men; are also married to men, and esteem that vnnaturale damnation an honor."*

Madagascar also delighted in dancing and singing boys dressed as girls. In the Empire of Dahomey I noted a corps of prostitutes kept for the use of the Amazon=soldieresses.

North of the Sotadic Zone, we find local, but notable instances. Master Christopher Burrough describes on the western side of the Volga "a very fine stone castle, called by the name Oueak, and adioyning to the same a Towne called by the *Russes, Sodom,* *** which was swallowed into the earth by the justice of God, for the wickednesse of the people." Again: although as a rule Christianity has steadily opposed pathologic love both in writing and preaching, there have been remarkable exceptions. Perhaps the most curious idea was that of certain medical writers in the Middle Ages: "In moderation the sexual use of boys is good for the health" (Tardieu). Bayle notices (under "Vayer") the infamous book of Giovanni della Casa, Archbishop of Benevento, *De laudibus Sodomiœ,* regularly known as *Capitolo del Forno.* The same writer refers to the report that the Dominican Order, which systematically decried *le vice,* had presented a request to the Cardinal di Santa Lucia that sodomy might be lawful during three months per annum, June to August; and that the Cardinal had underwritten the petition "Be it done as they demand." Hence the Fæda Venus of Bassista Mantovano. Bayle rejects the history for a curious reason, venery being colder in summer than in winter, and quotes the proverb "Avoid love-making, but drink deep in months without an R in them." But in the case of a celibate priesthood, such scandals are inevitable: witness the famous Jesuit epitaph Here lies a Jesuit, etc.

In our modern capitals, London, Berlin and Paris, for instance, the vice seems subject to periodical outbreaks. For many years, also, England sent her pederasts to Italy, and especially to Naples whence originated the term "The English Vice." It would be invidious to detail the scandals which of late years have startled the public in London and Dublin: for these the curious will consult the police reports. Berlin, despite her strong flavor of Phariseeism, Puritanism and Chauvinism in religion, manners and morals, is not a whit better than her neighbors. Dr. Gaspar, a well-known authority on the subject, adduces many interesting cases, especially an old Count Cajus and his six accomplices. Among his many correspondents one suggested to him that not only Plato and Julius Cæsar but also Winckelmann and Platen belonged to the society; and he had found it flourishing in Palermo, the Louvre, the Scottish Highlands and St. Petersburg, to name only a few places. Frederick the Great is said to have addressed these words to his nephew, "I can assure you from personal experience that it is an uncomfortable vice to cultivate." This suggests the popular anecdote of Voltaire and the Englishman who agreed upon an "experience" and found it far from satisfactory. A few days afterwards the latter informed the Sage of Ferney that he had tried it again and provoked the exclamation, "Once a philosopher: twice a sodomite!" The last revival of the kind in Germany is a society at Frankfort and its neighborhood, self-styled *Les*

Cravates Noires (Black ties) in opposition, I suppose, to
Les Cravates Blanches (white ties) of A. Belot.

Paris is by no means more depraved than Berlin and
London; but while the latter hushes up the scandal, French-
men do not: hence we see a more copious account of it
submitted to the public. For France of the seventeenth
century, consult the *Histoire de la Prostitution chez tous
les Peuples du Monde,* and *La France devenue Italienne,*
a treatise which generally follows *L'Histoire Amoureuse
des Gaules* by Bussy, Comte de Rabutin. The headquarters of male prostitution were then in the Champ Flory,
i.e., Champ de Flore, the privileged rendezvous of low
courtesans. In the seventeenth century, "when the dizzy-
headed Frenchman", as Voltaire sings, invented the term
"philosophers' sin," there was a temporary recrudescence;
and, after the death of Pidauzet de Mairobert (March
1779), his *Apologie de la Secte Anandryne* was published
in *L'Espion Anglais.* In those days the Allée des Veuves
in the Champs Elysées had a "space reserved for bug-
gers"—"veuve" (widow) in the language of Sodom being
the reigning mistress, the favorite youth.

At the decisive moment of monarchial decomposition
Mirabeau declares that pederasty was regulated and adds,
"The taste for Sodomy makes considerable gains, although
it is less fashionable than it was in the time of Henry III
(the French Heliogabalus), in whose reign men indulged
in mutual stimulation in the very entrance of the Louvre.
Paris is well known as the best-policed city in the world,
and as a result there are public places set aside for this
purpose. Youths destined for the profession are carefully
classified, for the bureaucratic system extends thus far.
They are examined, and those who can play both an
active and a passive role, who are good-looking, rosy-
cheeked, with nice plump figures, are reserved for the high

nobility or else obtain a good price from bishops and financiers. Those who have lost their testicles, or pulley-weights in the jargon of the trade (for our language is more chaste than our morals), but who can still give and receive, make up the second category. They are still expensive, because women use them in their active and men in their passive role. Those who are so worn out that they are no longer capable of an erection, although their sexual organs are complete, enter themselves as pathics pure and simple and comprise the third class. But the mistress of ceremonies makes sure that they really are impotent. The procedure is for them to lie on a mattress open at the bottom, while two whores caress the patient for all they are worth. A third gently beats the genitals with young stinging-nettles. After the test has gone on for a quarter of an hour, a long red pepper is thrust up the anus, and this causes a considerable irritation. Hot caudebec mustard is spread on the blisters made by the nettles and the glans is rubbed with camphor. Those who pass the test without showing the slightest sign of an erection are taken on as pathics at a third of the fee."

The Restoration and the Empire made the police more vigilant in matters of politics than of morals. The favorite club, which had its password, was in the rue Doyenne, old quarter St. Thomas des Louvre; and the house was a hotel of the seventeenth century. Two street doors, on the right for the male gynæceum and the left for the female, opened at 4 P.M. in winter and 8 A.M. in summer. A decoy-lad charmingly dressed in women's clothes, with big haunches and small waist, promenaded outside; and this continued till 1826 when the police put down the house.

Under Louis Philippe, the conquest of Algiers had evil results, according to the Marquis de Boissy. He complained unequivocally of Arab habits in French regiments, and declared that the result of the African wars was a dreadful wave of sodomy even as syphilis resulted from the Italian campaigns of that age of passion, the sixteenth century. From the military the scourge spread to civilian society, and the vice took such expansion and intensity that it may be said to have been democratized in cities and large towns; at least so we gather from the *Dossier des Agissements des Pédérastes*. A general gathering of *La Sainte Congrégation des glorieux Pédérastes* was held in the old Petite Rue des Marais where, after the theatre, many resorted under pretext of making water. They ranged themselves along the walls of a vast garden and exposed their podices: bourgeois, richards and nobles came with full purses, touched the part which most attracted them and were duly followed by it. At the Allée des Veuves, the crowd was dangerous from 7 to 8 P.M.: no policeman or night-watchman dared venture in it; cords were stretched from tree to tree and armed guards drove away strangers among whom, they say, was once Victor Hugo. This nuisance was at length suppressed by the municipal administration.

The Empire did not improve morals. Balls of sodomites were held at No. 8 Place de la Madeleine where, on January 2, 1864, some one hundred and fifty men met, all so well dressed as women that even the landlord did not recognize them. There was also a club for sotadic debauchery called the Cent Gardes and the Dragons de l'Impératrice. They copied the imperial toilette and kept it in the general wardrobe; hence *faire l'Impératrice* (play the Empress) meant to be used carnally. The site, a splendid hotel in the Allée des Veuves, was discovered by the Procureur-Général who registered all the names; but, as these belonged to not a few senators and dignitaries, the Emperor wisely quashed proceedings. The club was broken up on July 16, 1864. During the same year, *La Petite Revue,* edited by M. Loredan Larchy, son of the General, printed an article, "Refugees from Sodom": it discusses the letter of M. Castagnary to the Progrès de Lyons and declares that the vice had been adopted by whole sections of the Army. For its latest developments as regards the double-dealing of the *tantes* (pathics), the reader will consult the last issues of Dr. Tardieu's well-known *Etudes.* He declares that the servant class is most infected; and that the vice is commonest between the ages of fifteen and twenty-five.

The pederasty of *The Nights* may briefly be distributed into three categories.

The first is the funny form, as the unseemly practical joke of masterful Queen Budúr and the not less hardy jest of the slave-princess Zumurrud.

The second is in the grimmest and most earnest phase of the perversion, for instance where Abu Nowas debauches the three youths.

In the third form, it is wisely and learnedly discussed, to be severely blamed, by the Shaykhah or Reverend Woman.

To conclude this part of my subject, the enlightenment of obscene practices. Many readers will regret the absence from *The Nights* of that modesty which distinguishes "Amadis de Gaul"; whose author, when leaving a man and a maid together, says:

"And nothing shall be here related; for these and suchlike things which are conformable neither to good conscience nor nature, man ought in reason lightly to pass over, holding them in slight esteem as they deserve." Nor have we less respect for Palmerin of England who after a risqué scene declares, "Herein is no offense offered to the wise by wanton speeches, or encouragement to the loose by lascivious matter."

But these are not Oriental ideas and we must even take the Eastern as we find him. He still holds what exists in Nature cannot be wrong, together with "to the pure all things are pure"; and, as Bacon assures us the mixture of a lie doth add to pleasure, so the Arab enjoys the startling and lively contrast of extreme virtue and horrible vice placed in juxtaposition.

Those who have read through these ten volumes will agree with me that the proportion of offensive matter bears a very small ratio to the mass of the work. In an age saturated with cant hypocrisy, here and there a venal pen will mourn over the "pornography" of *The Nights,* dwell upon the "Ethics of Dirt" and the "Garbage of the Brothel"; and will lament the "wanton dissemination (!) of ancient and filthy fiction." This self-constituted *Censor morum* reads Aristophanes and Plato, Horace and Virgil, perhaps even Martial and Petronius, because "veiled in the decent obscurity of a learned language"; he allows men to speak Latin; but he is scandalized at stumbling blocks much less important in plain English. To be consistent, he must begin by bowdlerizing not only the classics, with which boys' and youths' minds and memories are soaked and saturated at schools and colleges, but also Boccaccio and Chaucer, Shakespeare and Rabelais; Burton, Sterne, Swift and a long list of works which are yearly reprinted and republished without a word of protest. Lastly, why does not this inconsistent Puritan purge the Old Testament of its allusions to human ordure and the pudenda, to carnal copulation and impudent whoredom, to adultery and fornication, to onanism, sodomy and bestiality? But this he will not do, the whited sepulcher! To the interested critic of the *Edinburgh Review* (No. 335 of

July 1886), I return my warmest thanks for his direct and deliberate falsehoods: lies are one-legged and short-lived, and venom evaporates. It appears to be that when I show to such men, so "respectable" and so impure, a landscape of magnificent prospects whose vistas are adorned with every charm of nature and art, they point their unclean noses at a little heap of muck here and there lying in a field corner.

One of the "little heaps of muck" in the magnificent landscape of the *Nights* that Burton mentions as occurring in the Old Testament is bestiality. Perhaps because of its comparative rarity as a vice he does not devote the space to it that he gives to sodomy, but as an anthropologist he was interested in the references to it that came his way. As a result there are quite a number of scattered footnotes concerning it throughout the many volumes of the *Nights*.

One has only to see the intense sexual activity of monkeys in a zoo to understand why the women of the *Nights* often believed that monkeys, and in particular the larger anthropoids such as the baboon, might be a source of exquisite sexual satisfaction—witness the happy reminiscence recounted during the course of the tale for the 471st night (Supplemental vol. v., p. 333): "The delight of that dog-faced baboon who deflowered me hath remained with me ever since." It might not be out of place here to recall the story (Vol. 4, p. 297) of the King's Daughter and the Ape:

There was once a Sultan's daughter, whose heart was taken with love of a black slave; he abated her maidenhead and she became passionately addicted to futtering, so that she could not do without it a single hour and complained of her case to one of her body-women, who told her that no thing poketh and stroketh more abundantly than the baboon. Now it so

72

chanced one day that an ape-leader passed under her lattice, with a great ape; so she unveiled her face and looking upon the ape, signed to him with her eyes, whereupon he broke his bonds and chain and climbed up to the Princess, who hid him in a place with her, and night and day he abode there, eating and drinking and copulating.

The same belief, Burton assures us, was also popular in Egypt; but he is certain that any women putting theory into practice would be doomed to disappointment and would derive little pleasure from the union. Thus, although in vol. 4, p. 297 of the *Nights* it is claimed that "no thing poketh and stroketh more strenuously than the Girs" (or hideous Abyssinian cynocephalus), Burton demolishes the claim in a footnote:

But it must be based upon popular ignorance: private parts of the monkey although they erect stiffly, like the priapus of Osiris when swearing upon his Phallus, are not of a girth sufficient to produce that friction which is essential to a woman's pleasure. I may here allude to the general disappointment in England and America caused by the exhibition of my friend Paul de Chaillu's Gorillas. He had modestly removed penis and testicles, the latter being somewhat like a bull's, and his squeamishness caused not a little grumbling and sense of grievance— especially among the curious sex.

There are a few references that I can trace in Burton's writings to male bestiality. One is very brief—just long enough, in fact, for him to recount one highly improbable

*The sequel to this story is, to my mind, one of the few really obscene passages in the *Nights*. E.L.

story. This apparent lack of interest is surprising, for he admits that, although bestiality is very rare in Arabia,

. . . it is fatally common among those most debauched of debauched races, the Egyptian proper and the Sindis. Hence the Pentateuch, whose object was to breed a larger population of fighting men, made death the penalty of lying with a beast. C. S. Sonnini (*Travels*, English translation, p. 663) gives a curious account of Fellah lewdness. "The female crocodile during congress is turned upon her back (?) and cannot rise without difficulty. Will it be believed that there are men who take advantage of the helpless situation of the female, drive off the male, and supplant him in this frightful intercourse? Horrible embraces, the knowledge of which was wanting to complete the disgusting history of human perversity!" The French traveler forgets to add the superstitious explanation of this congress, which is the sovereignest charm for rising to rank and riches.

It is difficult to know whether Burton really believed this extraordinary tale. The modern reader must wonder why the Fellah, if so desperate for sexual release and so short of women, did not resort to something simpler like masturbation rather than risk the anger of the supplanted male crocodile for the dubious joys of such a scaly embrace.

Of greater interest to Burton than the act of bestiality was the question of whether any issue was likely to result. He relates that "the Ajaib al-Hind tells a tale (ch. xxxix) of a certain Mohammed bin Bullishad who had issue by a she-ape: the young ones were hairless of body and wore quasi-human faces; and the father's sight had become dim by his bestial practice"; but it is clear that he was determined to keep an open mind on the subject. He returned to consideration of the problem in a footnote to the 558th Night, in vol. vi, p. 54:

In parts of West Africa and especially in Gorilla-land there are many stories of women and children being carried off by apes, and all believe that the former bear issue to them. It is certain that the anthropoid ape is lustfully excited by the presence of women. . . . The female monkey equally solicits the attention of man. . . . Whether there would be issue and whether such issue would be viable are still disputed points; the produce would add another difficulty to the pseudo-science called psychology, as such a mule would have only half a soul and issue by a congener would have a quarter soul. [This argument would seem to lie more in the field of theology than psychology. E.L.] A traveler well known to me proposed to breed pithecoid men who might be useful as hewers of wood and drawers of water: his idea was to put the highest races of apes to the lowest of humanity. I never heard what became of his "breeding stables."

It is a pity that he did not take the trouble to find out, for in another passage we find him appropriating the traveler's idea as a semi-established fact in an attempt to refute the categorical claims of scientists that no issue was possible from a union between man and beast:

Modern science which, out of the depths of its self-consciousness, has settled so many disputed questions, speaking by the organs of Messieurs Woodman and Tidy ("Medical Jurisprudence") has decided that none of the lower animals can bear issue to man. But the voice of the world is against them and as Voltaire says one cannot be cleverer than everybody. To begin with there is the will: the she-quandruman shows a distinct lust for man by fondling him and displaying her parts as if to entice him. That carnal connection had actually taken place cannot be doubted: my late friend Mirza Ali Akbar, of Bombay, the famous Munshi to Sir Charles Napier during the conquest of Sind, a man perfectly veracious and trustworthy, assured me that in the Gujarat province he had witnessed a case with his own eyes. He had gone out "to the jungle," as the phrase is, with another Moslem who, after keeping him waiting for an unconscionable time, was found carnally united to a she-monkey. My friend, indignant as a good Moslem should be, reproved him for his bestiality and then asked him how it had come to pass: the man answered that the she-monkey came regularly to look at him on certain occasions, that he was in the habit of throwing her something to eat and that her gratitude displayed such sexuality that he was tempted and "fell." That the male monkey shows an equal desire for women is known to every frequenter of the zoo. I once led a party of English girls to see a collection of mandrils and other anthropoid apes in the menagerie of a well-known Russian millionaire, near Florence, when the Priapism displayed was such that the girls turned back and fled in fright. In the motherlands of these anthropoids (the Gaboon, Malacca, etc.,) the belief is universal and women have the liveliest fear of them. In 1853 when the Crimean War was brewing, a dog-faced baboon in Cairo broke away from his Kuraydati (ape-leader), threw a girl in the street and was about to ravish her when a sentinel drew his bayonet and killed the beast. The event was looked upon as an evil omen by the older men, who shook their heads and declared that these were bad times when apes attempted to ravish the daughters of Moslems. But some will say that the grand test, the existence of the mule between man and monkey, though generally believed in, is characteristically absent, absent as the "missing link" which goes so far as to invalidate Darwinism in one and perhaps the most important part of its contention. Of course the offspring of such union would be destroyed, yet the fact of our never having found a trace of it except in legend and idle story seems to militate against its existence. When, however, man shall become Homo sapiens he will cast off the prejudices of the cradle and the nursery and will ascertain by actual experiment if human being and monkey can breed together. The lowest order of bimana, and the highest order of quadrumana may, under most favorable circumstances, bear issue and the "Mule," who would own half a soul, might prove most serviceable as a hewer of wood and a drawer of water, in fact as an agricultural laborer. All we can say is that such miscegenation stands in the category of things not proven and we must object to science declaring them non-existing. A correspondent favors me with the following note upon the subject:— Castanheda (*Annals of Portugal*) relates that a woman was transported to an island inhabited by monkeys and took up her abode in a cavern where she was visited by a huge baboon. He brought her apples and fruit and at last had connection with her, the result being two children in two to three years; but when she was being carried off by a ship the parent monkey kissed his progeny. The woman was taken to Lisbon and imprisoned for life by the King. Langius, Virgiliu Polydorus and others quote many instances of monstrous births in Rome resulting from the connection of women with dogs and bears, and cows with horses, etc. The following relative conditions are deduced on the authority of Mm. Jean Polfya and Mauriceau: 1. If the sexual organism of man or woman be more powerful than that of the monkey, dog, etc., the result will be a monster in the semblance of man; 2. if vice versa, the appearance will be that of a beast; 3. if both are equal the result will be a distinct subspecies as of the horse with the ass.

Even though this neat classification has no foundation in fact, Burton was undoubtedly right to keep an open mind on the subject. He was well aware that the history of science is littered with statements, categorically expressed, that have later been proved to be false; and at that time the science of genetics was insufficiently advanced for any proof to be forthcoming that Burton would have been prepared to accept.

3. Goa

In July 1846, at the age of twenty-five, Burton fell a victim to cholera and became very ill indeed. His recovery was extremely slow, and he was granted two years' sick leave in order to convalesce at Ootacamund in the healthy air of the Nilgiri Hills (in what was then southwestern Madras but is now the state of Kerala).

He traveled by sea from Bombay in a "pattimar" or native craft which he had hired. Ill though he had been, it was too much to expect that he would sail past a place so rich in historical associations as the little Portuguese colony of Goa. Camoes (the author of *The Lusiads*), Vasco da Gama, St. Francis Xavier—these names from Goa's history were a powerful attraction to a man who sought knowledge as avidly as Burton. He ordered the pattimar to put into Goa.

But Goa's glory lay in the past, and Richard Burton, visiting the ruined churches, the "desert aisles . . . the crowdless cloisters," found that "old Goa has few charms when seen by the light of day."

One of the charms that he did discover was a young teacher of Latin, "a very pretty white girl," in the old convent called Caza da Misericordia. He decided that she would be happier on British territory than among the elderly and plain-faced nuns of the convent. Accordingly, the young Lieutenant Burton made plans to carry her off, plans involving an imaginary young sister of his for whom he was allegedly seeking a suitable convent, and a servant called Allahdad to assist him in the abduction of the nun.

When, four years later, he came to write a book on Goa (*Goa, and the Blue Mountains: or Six Months' Sick Leave,* 1851) this scandalous attempted coup made too good a story to be left out, but he disguised it by making a Goanese named Salvador relate the tale to him as if it had been performed by another officer, and by changing his servant's name to Khudadad.

"About ten years ago," said Salvador, "I returned to Goa with my master, Lieut.——of the——Regiment, a very clever gentleman, who knew everything. He could talk to each man of a multitude in his own language, and all of them would appear equally surprised by, and delighted with, him. Besides, his faith was every man's faith. In a certain Musselmanee country he married a girl, and divorced her a week afterwards. Moreover, he chanted the Koran, and the uncircumcised dogs considered him a kind of saint. . . . Ah! he was a clever Sahib, that! he could send away a rampant and raging creditor playful as a little goat, and borrow more money from Parsees at less interest than was ever paid or promised by any other gentleman in the world.

"At last my master came to Goa, where of course he became so pious a Christian that he kept a priest in the house—to perfect him in Portuguese—and attended Mass once a day. And when we went to see the old city, such was the fervency of his lamentations over the ruins of the Inquisition, and the frequency of his dinners to the Padre of Saint Francis, that the simple old gentleman half canonized him in his heart. But I guessed that some trick was at hand when a pattimar, hired for a month, came and lay off the wharf stairs, close to where the Sahib is now sitting; and presently it appeared that my officer had indeed been cooking a pretty kettle of fish!

"My master had been spending his leisure hours with the Prioress of Santa Monica, who—good lady—when informed by him that his sister, a young English girl, was only waiting till a good comfortable quiet nunnery could be found for her, not only showed her new friend about the cloisters and dormitories, but even introduced him to some of the nuns. Edifying it must have been to see his meek countenance as he detailed to the Madres his well-digested plans for the future welfare of that apocryphal little child, accompanied with a thousand queries concerning the style of living, the moral and religious education, the order and discipline of the convent. The Prioress desired nothing more than to have an English girl in her house—except, perhaps, the monthly allowance of a hundred rupees which the affectionate brother insisted upon making to her.

"You must know, sahib, that the Madres are, generally speaking, by no means good-looking. They wear ugly white clothes, and cut their hair short, like a man's. But, the Latin professor . . . who taught the novices and the younger nuns learning, was a very pretty white girl, with large black eyes, a modest smile, and a darling of a figure. As soon as I saw that Latin professor's face, I understood the whole nature and disposition of the affair.

"My master at first met with some difficulty, because

81

the professor did not dare to look at him, and, besides, was always accompanied by an elder sister."

"Then, how did he manage?" . . .

. . . "Well, sahib . . . I told you that my master's known skill in such matters was at first baffled by the professor's bashfulness, and the presence of a grim-looking sister. But he was not a man to be daunted by difficulties: in fact, he became only the more ardent in the pursuit. By dint of labor and perseverance, he succeeded in bringing the lady to look at him, and being rather a comely gentleman, that was a considerable point gained. Presently her eternal blushings gave way, though occasionally one would pass over her fair face when my master's eyes lingered a little too long there: the next step in advance was the selection of an aged sister, who, being half blind with conning over her breviary, and deaf as a dead donkey, made a very suitable escort. . . . I was now put forward in the plot. After two days spent in lecturing me as carefully as a young girl is primed for her first confession, I was sent up to the nunnery with a bundle of lies upon my tongue, and a fatal necessity for telling them under pain of many kicks. I did it, but my repentance has been severe. . . .

"And, sahib, I also carried a present of some Cognac—called European medicine—to the prioress, and sundry similar little gifts to the other officials, not excepting the Latin professor. To her, I presented a nosegay, containing a little pink note, whose corner just peeped out of the chambeli (jessamine) blossoms. With fear and trembling I delivered it, and was overjoyed to see her presently slip out of the room. She returned in time to hear me tell the prioress that my master was too ill to wait upon them that day, and by the young nun's earnest look as she awaited my answer to the Superior's question concerning the nature of the complaint, I concluded that the poor thing

was in a fair way for perdition. My reply relieved their
anxiety. Immediately afterwards their curiosity came into
play. A thousand questions poured down on me, like the
pitiless pelting of the monsoon rain. My master's birth,
parentage, education, profession, travels, rank, age, fortune, religion, and prospects were demanded, till my brain
felt tired. According to instructions, I enlarged upon his
gallantry in action, his chastity and temperance, his love
for his sister, and his sincere devotion to the Roman
Catholic faith. . . . My allusion to the sister provoked
another outburst of inquisitiveness. On this subject, also, I
satisfied them by a delightful description of the dear little
creature, whose beauty attracted, juvenile piety edified,
and large fortune enchanted everyone. The eyes of the old
prioress glistened from behind her huge cheeks, as I dwelt
upon the latter part of the theme especially: but I remarked that the Latin professor was so little interested by
it, that she had left the room. When she returned, a book,
bound in dirty white parchment, with some huge letters
painted on the back of the binding, was handed over to
me for transmission to my master; who, it appears, had
been very anxious to edify his mind by perusing the life of
the holy Saint Augustine.

"After three hours spent in perpetual conversation, and
the occasional discussion of mango cheese, I was allowed
to depart, laden with messages, amidst a shower of bene-
dictions upon my master's head, prayers for his instant
recovery, and anticipation of much pleasure in meeting
him.

"I should talk till we got to Calicut, sahib, if I were to
detail to you the adventures of the ensuing fortnight. My
master passed two nights in the cloisters—not praying, I
suppose; the days he spent in conversation with the prioress and sub-prioress, two holy personages who looked

rather like Guzerat apes than mortal women. At the end of the third week a swift-sailing pattimar made its appearance.

"I was present when my master took leave of the Superior, and an affecting sight it was; the fervor with which he kissed the hand of his "second mother," his "own dear sister's protectress." How often he promised to return from Bombay, immediately the necessary preparations were made! How carefully he noted down the many little commissions entrusted to him! And, how naturally his eyes moistened as, receiving the benediction, he withdrew from the presence of the reverend ladies!

"But that same pattimar was never intended for Bombay; I knew THAT!

"My master and I immediately packed up everything. Before sunset all the baggage and the servants were sent on board, with the exception of myself, who was ordered to sit under the trees on the side of the wharf, and an Afghan scoundrel, who went out walking with the sahib about eleven o'clock that night. The two started, in native dresses, with their turbans concealing all but the parts about their eyes; both carried naked knives, long and bright enough to make one shake with fear, tucked under their arms, with dark lanterns in their hands. My master's face—as usual when he went on such expeditions—was blackened, and with all respect, speaking in your presence, I never saw an English gentleman look more like a Mussulman thief."

"But why make such preparations against a house full of unprotected women?"

"Because, sahib ... at night there are always some men about the nunnery. The knives, however, were only in case of an accident; for, as I afterwards learned, the Latin professor had mixed up a little datura seed with the tobacco served out to the guards that evening.

"A little after midnight I felt a kick, and awoke. Two men hurried me on board the pattimar, which had weighed anchor as the clock struck twelve. Putting out her sweeps she glided down the Rio swiftly and noiselessly.

"When the drowsiness of sleep left my eyelids I observed that the two men were my master and that ruffian Khudadad. I dared not, however, ask any questions, as they both looked fierce as wounded tigers, though the sahib could not help occasionally showing a kind of smile. . . . I was (later) favored with the following detail of his night's adventure.

"Exactly as the bell struck twelve, my sahib and his cutthroat had taken their stand outside the little door leading into the back garden. According to agreement previously made, one of them began to bark like a jackal, while the other responded regularly with the barking of a watchdog. After some minutes spent in this exercise they carefully opened the door with a false key, stole through the cloisters, having previously forced the lock of the grating with their daggers, and made their way toward the room where the Latin professor slept. But my master, in the hurry of the moment, took the wrong turning, and found himself in the chamber of the sub-prioress, whose sleeping form was instantly raised, embaced, and borne off in triumph by the exulting Khudadad.

"My officer lingered for a few minutes to ascertain that all was right. He then crept out of the room, closed the door outside, passed through the garden, carefully locked the gate, whose key he threw away, and ran toward the place where he had appointed to meet Khudadad, and his lovely burden. But imagine his horror and disgust when, instead of the expected large black eyes and the pretty little rosebud of a mouth, a pair of rolling yellow balls glared fearfully in his face, and two big black lips, at first shut with terror, began to shout and scream and abuse him with all their might.

" 'Khudadad, we have eaten filth,' said my master, 'How are we to lay this she-devil?"

" 'Cut her throat?' replied the ruffian.

" 'No, that won't do. Pinion her arms, gag her with your handkerchief, and leave her—we must be off instantly.'

"So they came on board, and we set sail as I have recounted to your honor."

"But why didn't your master, when he found out his mistake, return for the Latin professor?"

"Have I not told the sahib that the key of the garden gate had been thrown away, the walls cannot be scaled, and all the doors are bolted and barred every night as carefully as if a thousand prisoners were behind them?"

So Burton's attempt to rescue the damsel ended in failure. He now thought it best to complete his journey to Ootacamund where he continued his convalescence. After the investigations in Sind and the attempted abduction in Goa, he found the place dull and disagreeable and claimed it gave him "rheumatic ophthalmia." He passed the time in learning Persian, and in studying the local customs and religions. But these could not hold his interest for the full length of his sick leave, and in September 1847 he returned to Bombay, where he sat the official examination in Persian and passed out top. Though far from well, he persuaded the medical authorities that he was fit enough to return to duty.

Back in Karachi he plunged once again into native life, adding to the store of miscellaneous information that was to appear in that ragbag of a book, *Sindh, and the Races that Inhabit the Valley of the Indus,* from which we have already quoted.

In the spring of 1848 the second Sikh War broke out. Holding interpreter's certificates in six languages, the twenty-seven-year-old Burton applied for the post of interpreter for the army marching into West Punjab. But now his past caught up with him. To have set up a mess with a collection of monkeys in preference to messing with his fellow officers might have been regarded as eccentric: to have assigned the monkeys ranks, and to have put pearls in the ears of one of them and referred to it as his wife, might have given rise to speculation and gossip: but less forgivable in a society so rigidly conformist as the army was his predilection for staining himself with henna, donning native costume and, apparently, "going native." Inevitably this earned him the opprobrious title of "White Nigger." Such unorthodoxy might (just) have been overlooked in considering his application for the interpreter's post in view of his outstanding talents as a linguist; but when, on top of all this nonconformism, there lay in the Secretariat files in Bombay an incredibly detailed report on pederasty, the general suitability of Burton as an officer in the service of the Honourable East India Company was seriously questioned. The post was given to an officer knowing only one Indian language, and that not the language of the enemy the army was to meet.

Burton was shattered. His seven years of work were wasted. He was a failure. Up to now, arrogantly self-confident and impervious to criticism and to unpopularity, he had been master of his destiny: failure had been something that happened to other people. He could now see no further prospects for himself in India. Still not fully recovered from his bout of cholera, he obtained extended sick leave. From Karachi he traveled to Bombay, and from there sailed for England. Although he was to remain on the strength of the 18th Regiment of Bombay Native Infantry for another twelve years, he would not set foot in India again, except fleetingly, until 1876.

4. East Africa

The next four years were spent mostly in England and France. During this period Burton wrote two books on Sind, one on Goa, one on falconry, and a manual of bayonet exercises. He also planned the journey that was, perhaps, his greatest achievement.

In the autumn of 1852 he put forward a proposal for the exploration of central and eastern Arabia, including the Rub'al Khali. (Eighty years later in 1932, this vast expanse of desert, aptly named "the empty quarter," was crossed by H. St. John Philby, seven years after receiving from the Royal Asiatic Society the first Sir Richard Burton Memorial Medal. But even today the area remains largely unexplored.) The Royal Geographical Society was interested, but Burton's employers, the East India Company, refused their permission, regarding the project as being too dangerous. Instead, they granted Lt. Burton a year's leave to study Arabic. Typically, Burton utilized this year in doing just what he had wanted to do, involving a far more dangerous journey than that turned down by the

Court of Directors: he planned to visit the forbidden cities of Medina and Mecca.

Disguised once again as Mirza Abdullah, he joined the annual pilgrimage to these holy cities, knowing full well that the slightest mistake in language, thought, behavior or movement would send him to an almost certain and probably painful death. That he succeeded was a tribute to his courage, to his knowledge of the language, and to his deep understanding of the patterns of Arab thought. It was altogether a sensational exploit.

He returned to Cairo in September 1853, and there, uncharacteristically, idled away the rest of his leave. He now had to return to Bombay and to the dull prospect of regimental duty. In Bombay he wrote the three-volume account of his adventure, *Personal Narrative of a Pilgrimage to El-Medinah and Meccah,* and then devoted his thoughts to how he might avoid rejoining his regiment.

His solution was to propose an expedition to the ancient city of Harar—then in Somalia but now in Ethiopia—which no European had entered, though many had tried. It was a typical Burton project. Through the good offices of a friend, James Grant Lumsden, who was a member of the Bombay Council, approval for the expedition was obtained from the East India Company and Burton was granted the requisite leave.

With his selected companions he sailed from Bombay and arrived in Aden on October 1, 1854. A month was spent here in preparation for the exploration of the coastal areas of Somalia and for the dangerous journey to Harar. Burton's own preparations included the obtaining of whatever information he could, and from whatever sources, on Somalia and the Somalis. He discovered that among the few Somalis living in Aden were some prostitutes. From these he learned some interesting anthropological facts about female circumcision. Stored away in his memory or in notebooks, and added to by later reading and investigations, the information was to appear in a footnote to the "475th Night" of the *Arabian Nights* (vol. v, p. 279).

Moslems like the Classics (Aristotle and others) hold the clitoris (*Zambúr*) to be the seat and fountainhead of sexual pleasure which, says Sonnini, is mere profanity. In the babe it protrudes beyond the labiae and snipping off the head forms female circumcision. This rite is supposed by Moslems to have been invented by Sarah, who so mutilated Hagar for jealousy and was afterwards ordered by Allah to have herself circumcised at the same time as Abraham. It is now (or should be) universal in Al-Islam and no Arab would marry a girl "unpurified" by it. Son of an "uncircumcised" mother (Ibn al-bazrá) is a sore insult. As regards the popular idea that Jewish women were circumcised till the days of Rabbi Gersham (A.D. 1000) who denounced it as a scandal to the Gentiles, the learned Professor H. Graetz informs me, with some indignation, that the rite was never practiced and that the great rabbi contended only against polygamy. Female circumcision, however, is I believe the rule among some outlying tribes of Jews. The rite is the proper complement of male circumcision, evening the sensitiveness of the genitories by reducing it equally in both sexes: an uncircumcised woman has the venereal orgasm much sooner and oftener than a circumcised man, and frequent coitus would injure her health; hence I believe, despite the learned historian, that it is practiced by some Eastern Jews. "Excision" is universal among the Negroids of the Upper Nile (Werne), the Somal and other adjacent tribes. The operator, an old woman, takes up the instrument, a knife or razor blade fixed into a wooden handle, and with three sweeps cuts off the labia and the head of the clitoris. The parts are then sewn up with a packneedle and a thread of sheepskin; and in Dar-For a tin tube is inserted for the passage of urine. Before marriage, the bridegroom trains himself for a month on beef, honey and milk; and if he can open his bride with the natural weapon, he is a sworder to whom no woman in the tribe can deny herself. If he fails, he tries penetration with his fingers and by way of a last resort whips out his knife and cuts the parts open. The sufferings of the first few nights must be severe. The few Somali prostitutes who practiced at Aden always had the labia and clitoris excised and the skin showing the scars of coarse sewing. The moral effect of female circmcision is peculiar. While it diminishes the heat of passion it increases licentiousness, and breeds a debauchery of mind far worse than bodily unchastity because accompanied by a peculiar cold cruelty and a taste for artificial stimulants to "luxury." It is the sexlessness of a spayed canine imitated by the suggestive brain of humanity.

The sufferings of a Somali bride on her wedding night, owing to the barbarous rite of female circumcision, had no counterpart in the Western world; but Burton recognized that the average English girl often underwent on that first night an experience which, if it did not render her frigid, at least made it probable that she would never enjoy the act of sex. What made him so angry was that in most cases the shock and disgust felt by the bride arose from quite unnecessary ignorance on her part and thoughtlessness on the part of the husband.

Of course, a certain amount of pain appears to be fairly generally felt when virginity is lost. "Several women," writes Burton, "have described the pain to me as much resembling the drawing of a tooth." He was aware that loss of virginity does not necessarily occur on the wedding night (though it did so more often then that nowadays), but argued that the discomfort of defloration, when allied to considerable psychological distress, was frequently more than an innocent girl could take. Curiously, he has little to say about the different attitudes to defloration that existed in different countries, devoting only one short footnote to the subject. In the course of the tale told on the 351st night the youth was recounting how the girl "sat down beside me and bent lovingly over me and I rose up for her for I could no longer contain my passion and wrought that which was to be worked." This simple taking of a girl's virginity leads Burton to comment as follows:

The youth speaks of taking her maidenhead as if it were porter's work and so defloration was regarded by many ancient peoples. The old Nilotes incised the hymen before congress; the Phoenicians, according to Saint Athanasius, made a slave of the husband's abate it. The American Chibchas and Caribs looked upon virginity as a reproach, proving that the maiden had never inspired love. (For these and other examples see p. 72 Ch. vii., *L'Amour dans l'Humanité*, by P. Mantegazza, a civilized and unprejudiced traveler.)

It was not simply the discomfort attendant upon the rupturing of the hymen that caused so many English brides to dislike sexual intercourse. More important was their total ignorance of what to expect. Brides in the East, writes Burton, are informed about these things,

. . . but not in England, where mothers are idiots enough not to tell their daughters what to expect on the wedding night. Hence too often unpleasant surprise, disgust and dislike. The most modern form is that of the chloroformed bride upon whose pillow the bridegroom found a paper pinned and containing the words, *Mamma says you're to do what you like.* (Supplemental vol. 4, p. 42.)

Burton felt strongly about this deplorable and unnecessary ignorance of English and Continental brides, and he returned to the attack in Supplemental vol. 5, p. 223. In the 714th Night there occurs the passage, ". . . when the marriage-tie was tied the King went in unto her and found her like a pearl," the pearl signifying (as Burton explains in a footnote) something "that hath not been pierced." From this small platform he launched his attack on sexual ignorance caused by a misguided sense of delicacy.

"The first night," which is often so portentous a matter in England and upon the Continent (not of North America) is rarely treated as important by Orientals. A long theoretical familiarity with the worship of Venus

Leaves not much mystery for the nuptial night.

Such lore has been carefully cultivated by the "young person" with the able assistance of the ancient dames of the household of her juvenile companions and coevals and especially of the slave girls. Moreover not a few Moslems, even Egyptians, the most lecherous and salacious of men, in all ranks of life from prince to peasant take a pride in respecting the maiden for a few nights after the wedding feast extending, perhaps, to a whole week and sometimes more. A brutal haste is looked upon as "low"; and, as sensible men, they provoke by fondling and toying Nature to speak before proceeding to the final and critical act. In England it is very different. I have heard of brides over thirty years old who had not the slightest suspicion concerning what complaisance was expected of them: out of *mauvaise honte,* the besetting sin of the respectable classes, neither mother nor father would venture to enlighten the elderly innocents. For a delicate girl to find a man introducing himself into her bedroom and her bed, the shock must be severe and the contact of hirsute breast and hairy limbs with a satiny skin is a strangeness which must often breed loathing and disgust. Too frequently also, instead of showing the utmost regard for virginal modesty and innocence (alias ignorance), the bridegroom will not put a check upon his passions and precipitates matters with the rage of the bull, *ruentis in venerem*. Even after he hears "the cry" which, as the Arabs say, "must be cried," he has no mercy: the newly made woman lies quivering with mental agitation and physical pain, which not a few describe as resembling the tearing out of a back tooth, and yet he insists upon repeating the operation, never supposing in his stupidity that time must pass before the patient can have any sensation of pleasure and before the glories and delights of the sensual orgasm bathe her soul in bliss. Hence complaints, dissatisfaction, disgust, mainly caused by the man's fault, and hence not unfrequently a permanent distaste for the act of carnal congress. All women are by no means equally capable of such enjoyment, and not a few have become mothers of many children without ever being or becoming thoroughly reconciled to it. Especially in the case of highly nervous temperaments—and these seem to be increasing in the United States and notably in New England—the fear of nine months' pains and penalties makes the sex averse to the "deed of kind." The first child is perhaps welcomed, the second is an unpleasant prospect and there is a firm resolve not to conceive a third. But such conjugal chastity is incompatible, except in the case of "married saints" [that is, Mormons. Ed.] with a *bon ménage*. The husband, scandalized and offended by the rejection and refusal of the wife, will seek a substitute more complaisant; and the spouse also may "by the decree of Destiny" happen to meet the right man, the man for whom and for whom only every woman will sweep the floor. And then adieu to prudence and virtue, honor and fair fame. For, I repeat, it is the universal custom of civilized and Christian Europeans to plant their woman-kind upon a pedestal, exposed as butts to every possible temptation; and, if they fall, as must often be expected, to assail them with obloquy and contempt for succumbing to trails imposed upon them by the stronger and less sensitive sex. Far more sensible and practical, by the side of these high idealists, shows the Moslem who guards his jewel with jealous care and who, if his "honor," despite every precaution, insists upon disgracing him, draws the saber and cuts her down with the general approbation and applause of society.

At the end of October, in his disguise as an Arab merchant, Burton sailed from Aden and landed at Zeila on the coast of Somaliland. He remained there for a month, collecting guides, camels and food for the trek inland, and studying (among other things) the Somali women. In his subsequent account of the expedition to Harar, *First Footsteps in East Africa, or an Exploration of Harar* (published in 1856 and dedicated to his friend Lumsden), he wrote:

And now, dear L., I will attempt to gratify your just curiosity concerning *the* sex in Eastern Africa.

The Somali matron is distinguished—externally—from the maiden by a fillet of blue network or indigo-dyed cotton, which, covering the head and containing the hair, hangs down to the neck. Virgins wear their locks long, parted in the middle, and plainted in a multitude of hard thin pigtails: on certain festivals they twine flowers and plaster the head like Kafir women with a red ochre—the coiffure has the merit of originality. With massive round features, large flat craniums, long big eyes, broad brows, heavy chins, rich brown complexions, and round faces, they greatly resemble the stony beauties of Egypt—the models of the land ere Persia, Greece, and Rome reformed the profile and bleached the skin. They are of the Venus Kallipyga order of beauty: the feature is scarcely ever seen amongst young girls, but after the first child it becomes remarkable to a stranger. The Arabs have not failed to make it a matter of jibe.

> " 'Tis a wonderful fact that your hips swell
> Like boiled rice or a skin blown out,"

sings a satirical Yemeni: the Somal retort by comparing the lank haunches of their neighbors to those of the tadpoles or young frogs. One of their peculiar charms is a soft, low, and plaintive voice, derived from their African progenitors. Always an excellent thing in women, here it has an undefinable charm. I have often lain awake for hours listening to the conversation of the Bedouin girls, whose accent sounded in my ears rather like music than mere utterance.

In muscular strength and endurance the women of Somal are far superior to their lords: at home they are engaged all day in domestic affairs, and tending their cattle; on journeys their manifold duties are to load and drive the camels, to look after the ropes, and, if necessary, to make them; to pitch the hut, to bring water and firewood, and to cook. Both sexes are equally temperate from necessity; the mead and millet beer, so common among the Abyssinians and the Danakil, are entirely unknown to the Somal of the plains. As regards their morals, I regret to say that the traveler does not find them in the golden state which Teetotal doctrines lead him to expect. After much wandering, we are almost tempted to believe the bad doctrine that morality is a matter of geography; that nations and

97

races have, like individuals, a pet vice, and that by restraining one you only exasperate another. As a general rule Somali women prefer *amourettes* with strangers, following the well-known Arab proverb, "The new comer filleth the eye." In cases of scandal, the woman's tribe revenges its honor upon the man. Should a wife disappear with a fellow clansman, and her husband accord divorce, no penal measures are taken, but she suffers in reputation, and her female friends do not spare her. Generally, the Somali women are of cold temperament, the result of artificial as well as natural causes: like the Kafirs, they are very prolific, but peculiarly bad mothers, neither loved nor respected by their children. The fair sex lasts longer in eastern Africa than in India and Arabia: at thirty, however, charms are on the wane, and when old age comes on they are no exceptions to the hideous decripitude of the East.

The Somal, when they can afford it, marry between the ages of fifteen and twenty. Connections between tribes are common, and entitle the stranger to immunity from the blood-feud: men of family refuse, however, to ally themselves with the servile castes. Contrary to the Arab custom, none of these people will marry cousins; at the same time a man will give his daughter to his uncle, and take to wife, like the Jews and Gallas, a brother's relict. Some clans, the Habr Yunis for instance, refuse maidens of the same or even of a consanguineous family. This is probably a political device to preserve nationality and provide against a common enemy. The bride, as usual in the East, is rarely consulted, but frequent *têtes à têtes* at the well and in the bush when tending cattle effectually obviate this inconvenience: her relatives settle the marriage portion, which varies from a cloth and a bead necklace to fifty sheep or thirty dollars, and dowries are unknown. In the towns marriage ceremonies are celebrated with feasting and music. On first entering the nuptial hut, the bride-groom draws forth his horsewhip and inflicts memorable chastisement upon the fair person of his bride, with the view of taming any lurking propensity to shrewishness. This is carrying out wth a will the Arab proverb:

> The slave girl from her capture, the wife from her wedding.

During the space of a week the spouse remains with his espoused, scarcely ever venturing out of the hut; his friends avoid him, and no lesser event than a plundering party or dollars to gain would justify any intrusion. If the correctness of the wife be doubted, the husband on the morning after marriage digs a hole before his door and veils it with matting, or he rends the skirt of his Tobe, or he tears open some new hut-covering. Polygamy is indispensable in a country where children are the principal wealth.* The chiefs, arrived at manhood, immediately marry four wives: they divorce the old and unfruitful and, as among the Kafirs, allow themselves an unlimited number in peculiar cases, especially when many of the sons have fallen. Daughters, as usual in Oriental countries, do not "count" as part of the family: they are, however, utilized by the father, who disposes of them to those who can increase his wealth and importance. Divorce is exceedingly common, for the men are liable to sudden fits of disgust. There is little ceremony in contracting marriage

---

*I would advise polygamy among highly civilized races, where the sexes are nearly equal, and where reproduction becomes a minor duty. Monogamy is the growth of civilization: a plurality of wives is the natural condition of man in thinly populated countries, where he who has the largest family is the greatest benefactor of his kind.

with any but maidens. I have heard a man propose after half an hour's acquaintance, and the fair one's reply was generally the question direct concerning "settlements." Old men frequently marry young girls, but then the portion is high and the *ménage à trois* common.

The Somal know none of the exaggerated and chivalrous ideas by which passion become refined affection among the Arab Bedouins and the sons of civilization, nor did I ever hear of an African abandoning the spear and the sex to become a Darwaysh. Their "Hudhudu," however, reminds the traveler of the Abyssinian "eye-love," the Afghan's "Namzad-bazi," and the Semite's "Ishkuzri," which for want of a better expression we translate "Platonic love." This meeting of the sexes, however, is allowed in Africa by male relatives; in Arabia and central Asia it provokes their direst indignation. Curious to say, throughout the Somali country, kissing is entirely unknown.

At the end of November the expedition set out for Harar (some 170 miles as the crow flies to the southwest) and reached its destination early in the New Year. Burton was not impressed, either by the city or by its male inhabitants who, in his view, were ugly and often disfigured by disease. The women appeared beautiful by contrast, but the morals of both sexes left much to be desired:

The women, who, owing probably to the number of female slaves, are much and more numerous, appear beautiful by contrast with their lords. They have small heads, regular profiles, straight noses, large eyes, mouths approaching the Caucasian type, and light yellow complexions. Dress, however, here is a disguise to charms. A long, wide, cotton shirt, with short arms as in the Arab's Aba, indigo-dyed or chocolate-colored, and ornamented with a triangle of scarlet before and behind—the base on the shoulder and the apex at the waist—is girt round the

100

middle with a sash of white cotton crimson-edged. Women of the upper class, when leaving the house, throw a blue veil over the head, which, however, is rarely veiled. The front and back hair parted in the center is gathered into two large bunches below the ears and covered with dark blue muslin or network, whose ends meet under the chin. This coiffure is bound round the head at the junction of the scalp and skin by a black satin ribbon which varies in breadth according to the wearer's means: some adorn the gear with large gilt pins, others twine in it a Taj or thin wreath of sweet-smelling creeper. The virgins collect their locks, which are generally wavy not wiry, and grow long as well as thick, into a knot tied à la Diane behind the head: a curtain of short close plaits, escaping from the bunch, falls upon the shoulders, not ungracefully. Silver ornaments are worn only by persons of rank. The ear is decorated with Somali rings or red coral beads, the neck with necklaces of the same material, and the forearms with six or seven of the broad circles of buffalo and other dark horns prepared in western India. Finally, stars are tattooed upon the bosom, the eyebows are lengthened with dyes, the eyes fringed with Kohl, and the hands and feet stained with henna.

The female voice is harsh and screaming, especially when heard after the delicate organs of the Somal. The fair sex is occupied at home spinning cotton thread for weaving Tobes, sashes, and turbans; carrying their progeny perched upon their backs, they bring water from the wells in large gourds borne on the head; working in the gardens, and—the men considering, like the Abyssinians, such work as disgrace—they sit and sell in the long street which here represents the Eastern bazaar. Chewing tobacco enables them to pass much of their time, and the rich diligently anoint themselves with ghee, while the poorer classes use remnants of fat from the lamps. Their freedom of manners renders a public flogging occasionally indispensable. Before the operation begins, a few gourds of cold water are poured over their heads and shoulders, after which a single-thonged whip is applied with vigor.*

Both sexes are celebrated for laxity of morals.

After a return trek involving considerable hardship, Burton reached Aden in mid-February 1855. He returned to England, and immediately volunteered for active service in the Crimea, unaware that the Commander-in-Chief of the British forces, Lord Raglan, had no use at all for Indian Army officers. The East India Company granted him the necessary leave, and he sailed for the Crimea. He found a niche with a corps of Turkish irregular cavalry known as Beatson's Horse (their commander was a Colonel Beatson, of the Bengal Army). But the irregulars appeared to have created almost more problems than the enemy, and in the autumn Burton resigned in disgust and returned to England.

He now wrote his book, *First Footsteps in East Africa,* and gave serious consideration to further footsteps in the region in search of that philosophers' stone of African explorers, the source of the Nile. He also became engaged to a woman ten years younger than himself, Isabel Arundell.

During 1856 the plans for this new expedition matured. Support was forthcoming, and the East India Company granted Burton two years further leave on full pay. He sailed for Bombay, where he would obtain the necessary supplies, and on December 20th arrived at Zanzibar,

*When ladies are bastinadoed in more modest Persia, their hands are passed through a hole in a tent wall, and fastened for the infliction to a Falakah or pole outside.

which was to be the expedition's point of departure. But Burton was not a good administrator. He was far too egotistical to devote the time and attention that were required to the organization of an expedition of this importance. After various minor expeditions to the mainland, it was not until mid-June 1857 that he finally set off on his search for the lakes from which the Nile was believed to spring.

Of course, these six months were not wasted: they were merely not employed wholeheartedly in preparing for this major exploration. In his usual fashion Burton collected countless notes on the history, geography, ethnology, fauna, flora and climate of the island, and on the morals of its inhabitants. These were written up into a report which Burton sent addressed to the Royal Geographical Society of Great Britain. For some reason the report ended up in the Bombay branch of the Royal Asiatic Society, in whose strong box it lay for eight years. Hence it was not until 1872 that his book, *Zanzibar, City, Island, Coast,* based on the report, was published—two volumes and a thousand poorly written, badly arranged and often repetitious pages: it is not a good book. Burton claimed that "the white population of Zanzibar had in those days a great horror of publication," a horror sufficient to arrange for the diversion of his report from its destination. He may have been right: he did not think well of the population of Zanzibar:

The results of wealth and general complacence have been unbridled licentiousness. As usual in damp-hot climates—for instance, Sind, Egypt, the lowlands of Syria, Mazenderan, Malabar, and California—the sexual requirements of the passive exceed those of the active sex; and the usual result is a dissolute social state, contrasting with mountain countries, dry-cold or damp-cold, where

103

conditions are either equally balanced or are reversed. Arab women have been described as respectable in the Island because, fearing scandal and its consequences, they deny themselves to Europeans. Yet many of them prefer Banyans to those of the True Faith, whilst the warmest passions abandon themselves to African slaves: these dark men are such pearls in beauteous ladies' eyes, and their fascinations at Zanzibar are so great, that a respectable Hindustani Moslem will not trust his daughter to live there, even in her husband's house.

In an entirely pointless footnote, Burton adds:

It is easy to explain the preference of Arab women for slaves, and the predilection of the husbands for Negro women: the subject, however, is somewhat too physiological for the general reader.

But he had no such qualms regarding the private subscribers to the Burton Club. In a footnote (volume I, p. 6) to *The Arabian Nights* he explains the attraction more fully:

Debauched women prefer Negroes on account of the size of their parts. I measured one man in Somaliland who, when quiescent, numbered nearly six inches. This is a characteristic of the Negro race and of African animals; e.g., the horse; whereas the pure Arab, man or beast, is below the average for Europe; one of the best proofs, by the by, that the Egyptian is not an Asiatic, but a Negro partially whitewashed. Moreover, these imposing parts do not increase proportionally during erection; consequently, the "deed of kind" takes a much longer time and adds greatly to the woman's enjoyment. In my time no honest Hindi Moslem would take his womenfolk to Zanzibar on account of the huge attractions and enormous temptations there and thereby offered to them. Upon the subject of Imsak=retention of semen and "prolongation of pleasure," I shall find it necessary to say more.

This he does in yet another of his ubiquitous footnotes (*Arabian Nights*, vol. v, pp. 76, 77). It will perhaps be recalled that when Queen Zubaydah was bathing in the garden on a day of extreme heat, she was espied by the Caliph. "Presently, she became aware of him and turning, saw him behind the trees and was ashamed that he should see her naked. So she laid her hands on her parts, but the Mount of Venus escaped from between them, by reason of its greatness and plumpness." The sight so filled the Caliph with desire that he went away and asked the poet for some suitable verses. The poet obliged *ex tempore,* ending with a couplet to the delectable Mount of Venus: "Would heaven that I were on it, An hour, or better two hours, li'en." Burton remarks:

This leisurely operation of the "deed of kind" was sure to be noticed; but we do not find in *The Nights* any allusion to that systematic prolongation of pleasure which is so much cultivated by Moslems under the name *Imsák*=retention, witholding, i.e., the semen. Yet Eastern books on domestic medicine consist mostly of two parts; the first of general prescriptions and the second of aphrodisiacs, especially those which prolong the pleasure as did the Gaul by thinking of his poor mother. The *Ananga-Ranga,* by the Reverend Koka Pandit before quoted, gives a host of recipes which are used, either externally or internally, to hasten the paroxysm of the woman and delay the orgasm of the man. Some of these are curious in the extreme. I heard of a Hindi who made a candle of frogs' fat and fiber warranted to retain the seed till it

105

burned out: it failed notably because, relying on it, he worked too vigorously. The essence of the "retaining art" is to avoid overtension of the muscles and to preoccupy the brain: hence in coition Hindus will drink sherbet, chew betel nut and even smoke. Europeans, ignoring the science and practice, are contemptuously compared with village cocks by Hindu women who cannot be satisfied, such is their natural coldness, increased doubtless by vegetable diet and unuse of stimulants, with less than twenty minutes. Hence too while thousands of Europeans have cohabited for years with and have had families by "native women," they are never loved by them—at least I never heard of a case.

Before we leave the subject of the dimensions of the sexual organs of the males of various races, the reader may like to be reminded of the story told on the 584th Night of the *Arabian Nights*. This is the tale of a youth who went to the baths and stripped and the bathkeeper "saw not his yard, for that it was hidden between his thighs by reason of the excess of his fat, and there appeared thereof but what was like unto a filbert."

"This peculiarity," writes Burton in a footnote, "is not uncommon among the so-called Aryan and Semitic races, while to the Africans it is almost unknown. Women highly prize a conformation which (as the prostitute described it) is always " 'either in his belly or in mine.' "

However, the tale goes on to point the moral that not too much emphasis should be placed upon the apparent dimensions of the part when quiescent. The bathkeeper was highly amused by this minute object on a well-built youth, and so that his pretty wife might share in the amusement he introduced the youth to her and left them together. The couple were immediately attracted to each other and they embraced, "and the young man's yard swelled and rose on end, as it were that of a jackass, and he rode upon her breast and futtered her, whilst she sobbed and sighed and writhed and wriggled under him ..." And "she ceased not to abide with him till he had done his desire of her ten times running." Meanwhile the bathkeeper was listening to all this activity outside the locked door until he was beside himself with rage and frustration, whereupon he flung himself down from the roof and was killed.

But to return from the fiction of the *Nights* to the facts of Zanzibar. While the women preferred Negroes to their husbands, the men (by a satisfactory coincidence) preferred Negro women to their wives, but for a different reason:

A corresponding perversion and brutality of taste make the men neglect their wives for Negresses; the same has been remarked of our countrymen in Guiana and the West Indies, and it notably prevails in the Brazil, where Negresses and the Mulatta are preferred to the Creole. Considering the effect on the African skin when excited by joy, rage, fear, or other mental emotion, of course a cogent reason for the preference exists.

Later in the book, under the heading of "Racial Effluvium," Burton expands this reference as follows:

I am compelled by its high racial significance to offer a few words upon this unpleasant topic. The odor of the Wasawahili, like that of the Negro, is a rank fetor, peculiar to itself, which faintly reminded me of the ammoniacal smell exhaled by low-caste Hindus, popularly called Pariahs. These, however, owe it to external applications, aided by the want of cleanliness. All agree that it is most

107

offensive in the yellow-skinned, and the darkest Negroids are therefore preferred for domestic slaves and concubines. It does not depend upon diet. In the Anglo-American states, where blacks live like whites, no diminution of it has been remarked; nor upon want of washing—those who bathe are not less nauseous than those who do not. After hard bodily exercise, or during mental emotion, the epiderm exudes a fetid perspiration, oily as that of an orange peel: a Negro's feet will stain a mat, an oar must be scraped after he has handled it, and a woman has left upon a polished oaken gun case a hemispherical mark that no scrubbing could remove. This "Catinga," as the Brazilians call it, infects every part of the body with which it comes in contact, and exerts a curious effect on the white races. A missionary's wife owned to me in Zanzibar that it caused her almost to faint. I have seen an Englishman turn pale when he felt that a crowded slave craft was passing under his windows, and the late Sayyid [ruler] could not eat or drink for hours after he had been exposed to the infliction.

With "the darkest Negroids" available as domestic slaves it was unlikely that prostitution would be a lucrative occupation:

Public prostitutes here are few, and the profession ranks low where the classes upon which it depends can always afford to gratify their propensities in the slave market. I have alluded to the Wasawahili women of the Madagascar Quarter; a few also live scattered about the town, but all are equally undesirable—there is not a pretty face among them. The honorarium varies from 25¢ to $1, and the proceeds are expended upon gaudy dresses and paltry ornaments. Retired Corinthians who have not prospered live by fishing upon the sands, or make rude pottery at

Changani point: those who can afford it buy a slave or two, and give the rest of their days to farming. Girls who work for hire are always procurable, but such amours are likely to end badly: the same may be said of the prostitutes; consequently most white residents keep Abyssinian or Galla concubines.

Such concubinage did not, apparently, result in large numbers of unwanted children:

The domestic slave girl rarely has issue. This results partly from the malignant unchastity of the race, the women being so to speak in common: and on the same principle we witness the decline and extinction of wild tribes that come in contact with civilized nations. The chief social cause is that the "captive" has no interest in becoming a mother; she will tell you so in Brazil as in Zanzibar; her progeny by another slave may be sold away from her at any moment, and she obviates the pains and penalties of maternity by the easy process of procuring abortion.

In *The Arabian Nights* (vol. I, p. 27) Burton makes it clear that he does not approve of concubinage and that so far as he is concerned the system has only one redeeming feature:

Originally in Al-Islam the concubine (Surriyat, etc.) was a captive taken in war and the Koran says nothing about buying slave girls. But if the captives were true believers the Moslem was ordered to marry not to keep them. In modern days concubinage has become an extensive subject. Practically the disadvantage is that the slave girls, knowing themselves to be the master's property, consider him bound to sleep with them; which is by no means the mistress's view. Some wives, however, when old and childless, insist, after the fashion of Sarah, upon the husband taking a young concubine and treat her like a daughter—which is rare. . . . The only redeeming point in the system is that it obviated the necessity of prostitution which is, perhaps, the greatest evil known to modern society.

When Burton and his companion, John Hanning Speke, finally set out from Zanzibar on June 17, 1857, in their attempt to locate the source of the Nile, the preparations, as Burton admitted, "were hurriedly made." Thus the expedition was ill-prepared for the arduous task ahead of it: it was also ill-led, for Burton was far too self-centered to be a leader of men. His arrogance irritated his companion quite as much as Speke irritated him, until the two were hardly on speaking terms. Together they discovered Lake Tanganyika, a great achievement that should have reconciled the two men. But Speke was alone for the greater achievement, the discovery of Lake Victoria, and for this Burton never forgave him.

5. America

Back in England, while recovering his health after the innumerable attacks of fever contracted in East Africa and rigors of the exploration to Lake Tanganyika, Burton wrote his account of his travels: *The Lake Regions of Central Africa.* But he could not stay in England while Speke was the man of the hour and was busy preparing the expedition that would prove Lake Victoria to be the major source of the Nile. He applied for, and obtained, sick leave.

Most people apply for sick leave in order to rest and recuperate. Richard Burton used it to add to his vast store of experience and knowledge, to see new places, and, if necessary, to suffer new hardships. He did not even take the opportunity to get married, but set off to America, leaving his fiancée but a brief note of farewell, to see Salt Lake City, the city of the Mormons founded by Brigham Young in 1847.

He thoroughly enjoyed himself. He traveled by stage-coach, making copious notes on everything he saw. On red Indian women, for example:

Whilst the rich squaws rode, the poorer followed their packhorses on foot, eyeing the more fortunate as the mercer's wife regards what she terms the "carriage lady." The women's dress not a little resembles their lords"; the unaccustomed eye often hesitates between the sexes. In the fair, however, the waistcoat is absent, the wide-sleeved shift extends below the knees, and the leggings are of somewhat different cut. All wore coarse shawls, or white, blue, and scarlet cloth blankets around their bodies. Upon the Upper Platte we afterwards saw them dressed in cotton gowns, after a semi-civilized fashion, and with bowie knives by their sides. The grandmothers were fearful to look upon, horrid excrescences of nature, teaching proud man a lesson of humility, and a memento of his neighbor in creation, the "humble ape"—it is only civilization that can save the aged woman from resembling the gorilla. The middle-aged matrons were homely bodies, broad and squat like the African dame after she has become a mother; their hands and feet were notably larger from work than those of the men, and the burden upon their backs caused them to stoop painfully. The young squaws—pity it is that all our household Indian words, papoose, for instance, tomahawk, wigwam, and powwow, should have been naturalized out of the Abenaki and other harsh dialects of New England—deserve a more euphonious appellation. The belle savage of the party had large and languishing eyes and dentists' teeth that glittered, with sleek, long black hair like the ears of a Blenheim spaniel, justifying a natural instinct to stroke or pat it, drawn straight over a low, broad, Quadroon-like brow. Her figure had none of the fragility which distinguishes the higher race, who are apparently too delicate for human nature's daily food—porcelain, in fact, when pottery is wanted—nor had she the square corpulency which appears in the Negro woman after marriage. Her ears and neck were laden with tinsel ornaments, brass wire rings adorned her wrists and fine arms, a beadwork sash encircled her waist, and scarlet leggings, fringed and tasseled, ended in costly moccasins. When addressed by the driver in some terms to me unintelligible, she replied with a soft clear laugh—the principal charm of the Indian as of the smooth-throated African woman—at the same time showing him the palm of her right hand as though it had been a looking glass. The gesture would have had a peculiar significance in Sind; here, however, I afterwards learned, it simply conveys a refusal.*

He made inquiries about red Indian marriage customs:

Marriage is a simple affair with them. In some tribes the bride, as among the Australians, is carried off by force. In others the man who wants a wife courts her with a little present, and pickets near the father's lodge the number of horses which he supposes to be her equivalent. As among all savage tribes the daughter is a chattel, an item of her father's goods, and he will not part with her except for a consideration. The men are of course polygamists; they prefer to marry sisters, because the tent is more quiet, and much upon the principle with which marriage with a deceased wife's sister is advocated in England. The women, like the Africans, are not a little addicted to suicide. Before espousal the conduct of the weaker sex in many tribes is far from irreproachable. The "bundling" of Wales and of New England in a former day is not unknown to them, and many think little of that foretaste of marriage which, in the eastern parts of the New World, goes by the name of Fanny Wrightism and

*From *City of the Saints,* p. 73.

Free-loveism.* Several tribes make trial, like the Highlanders before the reign of James the Fifth, of their wives for a certain time—a kind of "hand-fasting," which is to Morality what Fetishism is to Faith. There are few nations in the world among whom this practice, originating in a natural desire not to "make a leap in the dark," cannot be traced. Yet after marriage they lead, like the Spartan matrons, a life of austerity in relation to the other sex. In cases of divorce, the children, being property, are divided, and in most tribes the wife claims the odd one. If the mother takes any care to preserve her daughter's virtue it is only out of regard to its market value. In some tribes the injured husband displays all the philosophy of Cato and Socrates. In others the wife is punished, like the natives of Hindustan, by cutting, or more generally by biting, off the nose tip. Some slay the wife's lover; others accept a pecuniary compensation for their dishonor and take as damages skins or horses. Elopement, as among the Arabs, prevails in places. The difference of conduct on the part of the women of course depends upon the bearing of the men. "There is no adulteress without an adulterer"— meaning that the husband is ever the first to be unfaithful— is a saying as old as the days of Mahommed. Among the Arapahos, for instance, there is great looseness; the Cheyennes on the contrary are notably correct. Truth demands one unpleasant confession, viz., on the whole, chastity is little esteemed among those Indians who have been corrupted by intercourse with whites.*

*Frances or Fanny Wright was born in Dundee in 1795. She emigrated to America and settled in New York, where she affronted large sections of American society by her lectures in which, among other things, she advocated a system of marriage based on moral obligations only. E.L.

*Op. cit. p. 142.

But what intrigued Burton most was the polygamic doctrine of the Mormons. Reaching Salt Lake City at the end of August 1860, he spent three weeks there, investigating the Mormon philosophy with his usual thoroughness. It was unusual, though, that his subsequent account of the plural marriage of the Mormon sect should be so temperate, so detached and so straightforwardly written. Burton had studied many religions and believed in none, so he could look at a religious belief in polygamy without prejudice: and since he always formed his own opinions and was uninterested in other people's, the hostility that Mormon polygamy aroused had no effect on him or on his thoughts. It would be hard to improve on the reasoned moderation of this account.

The first wife, as among polygamists generally, is *the* wife, and assumes the husband's name and title. Her "plurality" partners are called sisters—such as Sister Anne or Sister Blanche—and are the aunts of her children. The first wife is married for time, the others are sealed for eternity. Hence, according to the Mormons, arose the Gentile calumny concerning spiritual wifedom, which they distinctly deny. Girls rarely remain single past sixteen—in England the average marrying age is thirty—and they would be the pity of the community if they were doomed to a waste of youth so unnatural.

Divorce is rarely obtained by the man who is ashamed to own that he cannot keep his house in order; some, such as the President, would grant it only in case of adultery; wives, however, are allowed to claim it for cruelty, desertion, or neglect. Of late years, Mormon women married to Gentiles are cut off from the society of the Saints, and without uncharitableness, men suspect a sound previous reason. The widows of the Prophet are married to his successor, as David took unto himself the wives of Saul;

being generally aged, they occupy the position of matron rather than wife, and the same is the case when a man espouses a mother and her daughter.

It is needless to remark how important a part matrimony plays in the history of an individual, and of that aggregate of individuals, a people; or how various and conflicting has been Christian practice concerning it, from the double marriage, civil and religious, the former temporary, the latter permanent, of the Coptic or Abyssinian church, to the exaggerated purity of Mistress Anne Lee, the mother of the Shakers, who exacted complete continence in a state established according to the first commandment, increase and multiply. The literalism with which the Mormons have interpreted Scripture has led them directly to polygamy. The texts promising to Abraham a progeny numerous as the stars above or the sands below, and that "in his seed [a polygamist] all families of the earth shall be blessed," induce them, his descendants, to seek a similar blessing. The theory announcing that "the man is not without the woman, nor the woman without the man" is by them interpreted into an absolute command that both sexes should marry, and that a woman cannot enter the heavenly kingdom without a husband to introduce her. A virgin's end is annihilation or absorption, to sleep the sleep of everlasting night; and as baptism for the dead—an old rite, revived and founded upon the writings of St. Paul quoted in the last chapter—has been made a part of practice, vicarious marriage for the departed also enters into the Mormon scheme. Like certain British dissenters of the royal burgh of Dundee, who in our day petitioned Parliament for permission to bigamize, the Mormons, with Bossuet and others, see in the New Testament no order against plurality; and in the Old dispensation they find the practice sanctioned in a family, ever the friends of God, and out of which the Redeemer

116

sprang. Finally, they find throughout the nations of the earth three polygamists in theory to one monogamist.

The "chaste and plural marriage," being once legalized, finds a multitude of supporters. The anti-Mormons declare that it is at once fornication and adultery—a sin which absorbs all others. The Mormons point triumphantly to the austere morals of their community, their superior freedom from maladive influences, and the absence of that uncleanness and licentiousness which distinguish the cities of the civilized world. They boast that if it be an evil they have at least chosen the lesser evil, that they practice openly as a virtue what others do secretly as a sin—how full is society of these latent Mormons!—that their plurality has abolished the necessity of concubinage, cryptogamy, contubernium, celibacy, common-law marriages with their terrible consequences, infanticide, and so forth; that they have removed their ways from those "whose end is bitter as wormwood, and sharp as a two-edged sword." Like its sister institution Slavery, the birth and growth of a similar age, Polygamy acquires *vim* by abuse and detraction; the more turpitude is heaped upon it, the brighter and more glorious it appears to its votaries.

There are rules and regulations of Mormonism—I cannot say whether they date before or after the heavenly command to pluralize—which disprove the popular statement that such marriages are made to gratify licentiousness, and which render polygamy a positive necessity. All sensuality in the married state is strictly forbidden beyond the requisite for ensuring progeny—the practice, in fact, of Adam and Abraham. During the gestation and nursing of children, the strictest continence on the part of the mother is required—rather for a hygienic than for a religious reason. The same custom is practiced in part by the Jews, and in whole by some of the noblest tribes of savages; the splendid physical development of the Kaffir

117

race in South Africa is attributed by some authors to a rule of continence like that of the Mormons, and to a lactation prolonged for two years. The anomaly of such a practice in the midst of civilization is worthy of a place in Balzac's great repertory of morbid anatomy; it is only to be equaled by the exceptional nature of the Mormon's position, his past fate and his future prospects. Spartan-like the Faith wants a race of warriors, and it adopts the best means to obtain them.

Besides religious and physiological, there are social motives for the plurality. As in the days of Abraham, the lands about New Jordan are broad and the people few. Of the three forms that unite the sexes, polygamy increases, while monogamy balances, and polyandry diminishes, progeny. The former, as Montesquieu acutely suggested, acts inversely to the latter by causing a preponderance of female over male births. "An important and noteworthy fact," says M. Rémy, "is that in Utah female births outnumber male the reverse of the situation observed in countries in which monogamy holds sway, but in perfect conformity with what has been observed among Moslem polygamists." M. Rémy's statement is as distinctly affirmed by Mr. Hyde, the Mormon apostate. In the East, where the census is unknown, we can judge of the relative proportions of the sexes only by the families of the great and wealthy, who invariably practice polygamy, and we find the number of daughters mostly superior to that of sons, except where female infanticide deludes the public into judging otherwise. In lands where polyandry is the rule—for instance, in the Junsar and Bawar parganas of the Dhun—there is a striking discrepancy in the proportions of the sexes among young children as well as adults; thus, in a village where 400 boys are found there will be 120 girls, and on the other hand, in the Gurhwal Hills, where polygamy is prevalent, there is a surplus of female children. The experienced East Indian official who has published this statement is "inclined to give more weight to nature's adaptability to national habit than to the possibility of infanticide," for which there are no reasons. If these be facts, Nature then has made provision for polygamy and polyandry: our plastic mother has prepared her children to practice them all. Even in Scotland modern statistics have observed that the proportion of boys born to girls is greater in the rural districts; and attributing the phenomenon to the physical weakening of the parents, have considered it a rule so established as to "afford a valuable hint to those who desire male progeny." The anti-Mormons are fond of quoting Paley: "It is not the question whether one man will have more children by five wives, but whether these five women would not have had more children if they had each had a husband." The Mormons reply that—setting aside the altered rule of production—their colony, unlike all others, numbers more female than male immigrants; consequently that, without polygamy, part of the social field would remain untilled.

To the unprejudiced traveler it appears that polygamy is the rule where population is required, and where the great social evil has not had time to develop itself. In Paris or London the institution would, like slavery, die a natural death; in Arabia and in the wilds of the Rocky Mountains it maintains a strong hold upon the affections of mankind. Monogamy is best fitted for the large, wealthy, and flourishing communities in which man is rarely the happier because his quiver is full of children, and where the mistress becomes the substitute for the "plurality-wife." Polyandry has been practiced principally by priestly and barbarous tribes who fear most for the increase of their numbers, which would end by driving them to honest industry. It reappears in a remarkable manner in the highest state of social civilization, where excessive expenditure is an obstacle to freehold property, and the practice is probably on the increase.

The other motive for polygamy in Utah is economy. Servants are rare and costly; it is cheaper and more comfortable to marry them. Many converts are attracted by the prospect of becoming wives, especially from places where, like Clifton, there are sixty-four females to thirty-six males. The old maid is, as she ought to be, an unknown entity. Life in the wilds of western America is a course of severe toil: a single woman cannot perform the manifold duties of housekeeping, cooking, scrubbing, washing, darning, childbearing, and nursing a family. A division is necessary, and she finds it by acquiring a sisterhood. Throughout the States whenever a woman is seen at manual or outdoor work, one is certain that she is Irish, German, or Scandinavian. The delicacy and fragility of the Anglo-American female is at once the cause and the effect of this exemption from toil.

The moral influence diffused over social relations by the presence of polygamy will be intelligible only to those who have studied the working of the system in lands where seclusion is practiced in its modified form, as among the Syrian Christians. In America, society splits into two parts—man and woman—even more readily than in England, each sex is freer and happier in the company of its congeners. At Gt. S. L. City there is a gloom, like that which the late Professor H. H. Wilson described as being cast by the invading Moslem over the innocent gaiety of the primitive Hindu. The choice egotism of the heart called Love—that is to say, the propensity elevated by sentiment, and not undirected by reason—subsides into a calm and unimpassioned domestic attachment: romance and reverence are transferred, with the true Mormon concentration, from Love and Liberty to Religion and the Church. The consent of the first wife to a rival is seldom refused, and a *ménage à trois,* in the Mormon sense of the phrase, is fatal to the development of that tender tie which must be confined to two. In its stead there is household comfort, affection, circumspect friendship, and domestic discipline. Womanhood is not petted and spoiled as in the Eastern states; the inevitable cyclical revolution, indeed, has rather placed her below par, where, however, I believe her to be happier than when set upon an uncomfortable and unnatural eminence.

It will be asked what view does the softer sex take of polygyny? A few, mostly from the old country, lament that Mr. Joseph Smith ever asked of the Creator that question which was answered in the affirmative. A very few, like the Elected Vessel, Emma, the first wife of Mr. Joseph Smith—who said of her, by-the-by, that she could not be contented in heaven without rule—apostatize, and become Mrs. Bridemann. The many are, as might be expected of the easily molded weaker vessel, which proves its inferior position by the delicate flattery of imitation, more in favor of polygyny than the stronger.

For the attachment of the women of the Saints to the doctrine of plurality there are many reasons. The Mormon prophets have expended all their arts upon this end, well knowing that without the hearty cooperation of mothers and wives, sisters and daughters, no institution can live long. They have bribed them with promises of Paradise—they have subjugated them with threats of annihilation. With them, once a Mormon always a Mormon. I have said that a modified reaction respecting the community of Saints has set in throughout the States; people no longer wonder that their missionaries do not show horns and cloven feet, and the federal officer, the itinerant politician, the platform orator, and the place-seeking demagogue, can no longer make political capital by bullying, oppressing and abusing them. The tide has turned, and will turn yet more. But the individual still suffers: the apostate Mormon is looked upon by other people as a scamp or a knave, and the woman worse than a prostitute. Again, all the fervor of a new faith burns in their bosom with a heat which we can little appreciate, and the revelation of Mr. Joseph Smith is considered on this point as superior to the Christian as the latter is in others to the Mosaic Dispensation. Polygamy is a positive command from heaven: if the flesh is mortified by it so much the better—"No Cross, no Crown"; "Blessed are they that mourn." I have heard these words from the lips of a well-educated Mormon woman who, in the presence of a Gentile sister, urged her husband to take unto himself a second wife. The Mormon household had been described by its enemies as a hell of envy, hatred and malice—a den of murder and suicide. The same has been said of the Moslem harem. Both, I believe, suffer from the assertions of prejudice or ignorance. The temper of the new is so far superior to that of the old country, that, incredible as the statement may appear, rival wives do dwell together in amity; and do quote the proverb "the more the merrier." Moreover, they look with horror at the position of the "slavey" of a pauper mechanic, at being required to "nigger it" upon love and starvation, and at the necessity of a numerous family. They know that nine-tenths of the miseries of the poor in large cities arise from early and imprudent marriages, and they would rather be the fiftieth "sealing" of Dives than the toilsome single wife of Lazarus. The French saying concerning motherhood—"the first beautifies, the second destroys, the third completes the ruin."— is true in the Western world. The first child is welcomed, the second tolerated, the third is the cause of tears and or some similar monstrosity, with disgust and hatred of reproaches, and the fourth, if not prevented by gold pills, the cause. What the Napoleonic abolition of the law of primogeniture, combined with centralization of the peasant class in towns and cities, has effected on this side of the Channel, the terrors of maternity, aggravated by a highly nervous temperament, small cerebellum, constitutional frigidity and extreme delicacy of fiber, have brought to pass in the older parts of the Union.

Another curious effect of fervent belief may be noticed in the married state. When a man has four or five wives with reasonable families by each, he is fixed for life: his interests, if not his affections, bind him irrevocably to his New Faith. But the bachelor, as well as the monogamic youth, is prone to backsliding. Apostasy is apparently so common that many of the new Saints form a mere floating population. He is proved by a mission before being permitted to marry, and even then women, dreading a possible renegade with the terrible consequences of a heavenless future to themselves, are shy of saying yes. Thus it happens that male celibacy is mixed up in a curious way with polygyny: and that also in a faith whose interpreter advises youth not to remain single after sixteen, nor girls after fourteen. The celibacy also is absolute; any infraction of it would be dangerous to life. Either then the first propensity of the phrenologist is poorly developed in these lands—this has been positively stated of the ruder sex in California—or its action is to be regulated by habit to a greater degree than is usually believed.

In *The City of the Saints,* Burton then goes on to quote a remarkable letter from a Mormon wife, Mrs. Belinda Pratt, which explains with patience and at great length the scriptural bases of the Mormon belief in a plurality of wives. It is well worth reading, but it would be out of place to quote it here.

Now that he was knowledgeable about polygamy, Burton was to return to the subject in many brief references in future books, and once at length. This will be quoted in due course.

He now turned his steps homeward. Traveling via Panama, he reached England in time for Christmas, and on January 22, 1861 he married Isabel Arundell. He was almost forty.

6. Nigeria

His life now changed in more ways than one. Hard on the heels of his marriage came the news that his name had been deleted from the rolls of the 18th Regiment of Bombay Native Infantry: after nineteen years he was no longer an officer of the Indian Army. Having gained a wife, he had lost a job, an income and a pension. He had virtually no financial resources.

He therefore had little alternative but to accept the post that was offered to him, designed as it might have been for the disposal of difficult people like Burton: the consulship at Fernando Po.

Fernando Po is a very small island tucked into the steamy armpit of West Africa. It lies almost on the Equator in the Bight of Biafra, which itself is in the Gulf of Guinea. Swarming with malarial mosquitoes, it was not a healthy place. If Burton had been an ordinary man his chances of survival would have been few; but being the man he was, he increased these chances by the simple device of spending very little time on the island. He had found that his jurisdiction covered the Bight of Biafra.

Without consulting anyone, he extended it as far north as Dahomey and as far south as Angola, and thus obtained a good slice of Africa to explore.

He had only been on Fernando Po two weeks before setting out as a self-elected member of a small diplomatic mission to Abeokuta on the Ogun River in western Nigeria. As usual he made detailed observations and notes which were later written up at length into a two-volume book, *Abeokuta and the Cameroons.* Traveling upriver, the party arrived one night at the village of Baragu, where Burton had the opportunity to study the natives of the Egba race. He was struck by the fine figures of the people, and confidently attributed them to the practice of polygamy.

The women consider elongated bosoms a charm, and even the men show flaccid mammary glands. This "bestial exposure of the sacred part of a woman's form," as some term it, first disappears among the Moslem converts from heathenry. The goodwives had little remarkable, save a plug of pipestem-shaped coral worn in the left nostril: it may serve the purpose of the Indian nose ring. Many of them wore their hair upstanding in little tufts of wool, which coiffure, says a German traveler, "made them look more like horned fiends than human beings." Some of the tattooes were painfully ugly—lines of scars and dreadful knobs and marbles raised in highest relief by some encaustic process. Severe scalds were common; and one woman had her back adorned with what appeared to be an imitation in thickened skin of gouts and streamlets of blood. . . .

This race—the Egbado or Lower Egba—is distinctly Negroid, without showing the characteristics of the full-blooded Negro. . . . The lips are not thick, but the gums are blue, and the teeth are by no means improved by the process of chewing. One cannot, however, but be struck by the contrast between the prognathous, chinless, retreating face, simulating the Simiadae, and the admirable forms and figures of the people, who compare most favorably with those of the xanthous complexion. Their diet is poor, their climate poorer; callisthenics are unknown; they are not boxers or runners, like the people of Nupe; and even gymnastics, except tumbling, are little practiced. What then can account for the beauty of their conformation?

For my part I must attribute it to the almost invariable custom which the savage man possesses, and which his civilized brother abandons. Among ancient races, such as the Hebrew and the Persian, it was the rule of religion for the husband to separate from his wife during the period of gestation and lactation. A modified monogamy among the Greeks and Romans introduced abuses which the nations of the barren north, especially those of Europe, who cannot afford a plurality of wives, have perpetuated. On the coast and in the interior of Africa the instinctive law of nature is almost universally obeyed, and the people are necessarily polygamous. Speaking of Mandenga-land, Mungo Park says, "Three years" nursing is not uncommon; and during this period the husband devotes his whole attention to his other wives." In Hausa, as in Yoruba, the period of lactation extends to the third year. The West African and the Kaffirs of the southern continent practice this abstinence. and prove in their persons the beneficial effects of it. Europeans, violating the order of the animal creation, lay to their souls the flattering unction that they are the largest and the strongest of races, forgetting that by conforming to this African custom they might become both larger and stronger. Besides, it would necessitate polygyny—that is to say, a love of offspring warmer than sexual feeling. The Mormons have tried it with success; and to the excellent letter of Mrs. Belinda Pratt I must refer the reader for more information upon this momentous subject than could be conveyed in these pages.*

Never averse to digressing, nor to riding a hobbyhorse, Burton does both in a chapter entitled "Touching Matters Religious at Abeokuta." A brief description of the marriage rites of the Egbas is sufficient to launch him into what was now his pet subject: polygamy. It is not known how his wife felt about his obvious approval of the custom.

There is nothing remarkable in the marriage rites of the Egbas. Betrothal takes place early, although the girl is rarely married before eighteen or twenty, and the dowry, among the middle classes, may be four dollars. The bride and bridegroom repair to Ife, or some other place of pilgrimage; pray, and sacrifice. At night the bridesmaids escort the bride to her new home, where a feast leads to the consummation of the marriage. If the groom be satisfied, he sends presents to the wife's family, especially to his mother-in-law, who is called the "little mother," in contradiction to the true parent. If he finds reason to complain, he dismisses his bride and sends, bitterly, a few

---

*In a footnote to "polygyny" Burton tells the following story: When the late king, Eyo Honesty, of Old Calabar River, resolved to adopt the single wife system, the chosen one determined on a certain occasion to act as if she had been a unit in the normal score. Mrs W——, the wife of one of the Scotch Presbyterian missionaries, was directed—when the husband laid his complaint before them—to call upon the queen, and to bring her majesty to a finer sense of her conjugal duties. The labor of love was, however, I believe in vain.

broken cowries to her mamma. The marriages are not very prolific; "fecundity diminishes in proportion as we advance from temperate regions to the pole and the equator." All Africans—among whom there is a curious Malthusian instinct—possess anaphrodisiacs, and, finally, the prolonged lactation, by determining the vital current to the breast, prevents the women from becoming mothers. There are few ceremonies after birth: a name is presently given to the child, and, as among the Mpongwe of the Gaboon River, water is sprinkled on it—a faint resemblance to the modern, not the ancient, baptism of the Christians. The son inherits all the father's wives save his own mother.

Polygamy is, of course, the foundation stone of Yoruban society. I cannot remember a single African or Asiatic tribe—except the polyandrous—in which this is not the case, and the rule is equally applicable to the North American aborigines. Europe forms, and almost always has formed, the sole exception. To account for this fact perhaps a few lines may not be out of place.

The savage and the barbarian are polygamic because they are dependent for the necessaries and for the little comforts of their poor existence upon a plurality of women and the number of their children. Servants are unknown; slaves are rare. A single wife cannot perform all the offices required even in the simplest stage of society. Moreover, there is, in the different races of sub-species of mankind, as among the humbler animals, a greater or lesser difference, bodily and mental, between the two sexes. In the gallinaceae the male is far nobler than the female; in the equines the two are nearly equal; in the falconidae the female is stronger and braver than the male. Thus, in the European and the Hindu, the woman is quasi-equal with the man; in the African, the American,

and the lower races of Asiatic, she is inferior and monoga-
mous, while his propensities are polygamic.*

Among the Jews there was at first no attempt at the
vulgar limitations of the family. "The care of the Mosaic,
as of other Oriental legislation, was directed to the protection of the woman from harsh behavior or capricious
desertion, and to the fair treatment of the offspring without reference to the mutual affection of the parents. That
the man who associated with a virgin incurred the charge
of her protection, and that the mother, by the very act of
maternity, assumed the lesser dignity of the wife, were the
foundations of the domestic morals of the ancient world,
the guiding principles of the social life."†

*The Hindu race, in early times, made an approximation
to monogamy. The country was then almost civilized, and the
population must have been dense. The Semitic family shows
the same phenomenon. But when quoting the words of the
Eastern poet—

> His wives may never be four,
> He will best consult his reason,
> Best secure his home from treason,
> Who takes one, and wants no more—

they should be read rather as a grumble against the "legalities
and proprieties of society" than as a theory which could be
generally carried out. The Asiatic races that are inferior to
the Arab and the Hindu have never, I believe, adopted
monogamy, though polyandry has been practiced for centuries.

†I have borrowed these sentences, and almost all the
information contained in these paragraphs, from a Paper in
the *Edinburgh Review,* January 1862. The reader will readily
recognize the master-hand in that admirable article. It is
amusing, however, to see in it what a poor halfpenny-worth

130

Samuel and the Patriarchs had two or more spouses,
Solomon had a countless harem, as became a king of
kings, and Cato looked upon his wife merely as a machine

there is of bread (monogamy) to an intolerable deal of sack
(polygamy). Whilst pages 19, 20, 21, 22, and 23 are devoted
to showing that polygamy was a Mosaic institution, unforbid-
den to the early Christians, and only rendered restrictive and
penal—principally by the Church of Rome—in modern times,
a single sentence informs us that the settlement of the
question was left to old Roman laws, to German manners,
and to "the silent but absolute operation of a religion, based
on the sentiments with which no system of polygamy seems
to be compatible—freedom and love."

An eminent Moslem divine—El Siyuti, I think—wrote a
Moslem treatise on what to avoid. Through some three
hundred pages he indulges his reader with a full description
of the most voluptuous practices of the East—a perfect
worship of Bacchus and Venus. In the last he perorates,
beginning—"This much, O reader, have I recounted unto thee,
so that thou mayest know the things forbidden unto thee,"
etc., etc.

With respect to the reviewer's last assertion, viz., that
Christianity is based upon freedom and love—I doubt that
the monogamic sentiment was ever intended by it. And I
doubt even more vehemently whether the mixture of sentiment and passion, which we know by that name, has not
added to the miseries rather than conduced to the happiness
of human life. In my humble opinion, it is not one of the
least merits of polygamy that it abstracts from the parents an
affection which it bestows upon the progeny. As no man, it is
said, can serve God and Mammon, so no woman can equally
love husband and children; even the same woman, at different periods of her existence, will prefer one to the detriment
of the other. And while conjugal love contains the base alloy
of sexual feeling, parental affection is of all the most pure
and holy. The unselfish will find no difficulty in pointing out
which to prefer.

131

for the manufacture of progeny. As society became more complex, a certain limitation became necessary. The customary laws of the Jews confined the high priest to one wife, and apostolic injunction continued the same to the Christian bishop, without, however, forbidding a plurality of wives to the laity or to the other officers of the Church. It is hard to believe that this want of express condemnation arose from mere expediency, from the danger of disruption of the Oriental home, and from the fear of its being an obstacle to the conversion of the wealthier classes. Those familiar with the modes of thought in the East well know the horror and loathing with which the people generally look upon the one-wife system, their contempt for the bastard, and their inability to witness in their own society those scenes which the monogamic cities of Europe must tolerate for fear or even greater social evils to the family. The ordinary Hebrew was ordered to be content with four wives, a practice perpetuated by the apostle of El Islam, and the king to eighteen. Thus Josephus distinctly called polygamy "the custom of his country." Nor was it modified till the depression of the Jew's social position compelled him to follow the laws and customs of the nations among whom he was located. "In the eleventh century Rabbi Gerson, in connection with other Jewish doctors in France and the north of Germany, prohibited marrying more than one wife under pain of excommunication, and this was afterwards accepted by most European congregations. Nevertheless, both in Italy and Germany there seems to have existed the permission to take a second wife, when the first was hopelessly barren, and Papal dispensations to this effect are recorded to have been given in the dominions of the Holy See as late as the seventeenth century (*vide Historia degli riti Hebraici,* by Leo. Mutensis, 1657, cited by Selden in his *Uxor Hebrai-*

ci); while in Sicily, where the Saracenic traditions might still linger, the author of the *Ebraismo della Sicilia,* writing in 1748, attributes the rapid increase of the Jewish population to the enforced early marriages and the habitual practice of polygamy." (*Inquisator Reale della suprema Inquisizione di Sicilia,* by Giovanni de' Giovanni, p. 20.)*

It is, as the reviewer well remarks, entirely gratuitous to

---

*St. Augustine, Grotius, and other authorities admit that polygamy is more natural than monogamy, yet they declare—and they are followed by Paley—that it would prevent an increase of population. The contrary is the case. Hippocrates, Harvey, Willoughby, Forster, and the practice of the Mormons, show that among all animals, mankind included, polygamy tends to population by increasing the births of female children. Dr. Johnson (*Life,* vol. iii., p. 71), says it is "not natural for a man and a woman to live together in the married state." Balzac explains this by observing that "physically and morally, man is man longer than woman is woman." Napoleon, the list of the three Avataras of intellect, declares, in the *Code Civile,* "Marriage is not drawn from Nature."

In the *City of the Saints,* I flattered myself it had been proved that whereas monogamy equalizes the birth of the two sexes, polygamy produces more females, and polyandry more males. Hence came the deduction that "Nature, our plastic mother, had prepared her children for all three systems." The *British Quarterly Review,* of January 1, 1862, in an un-able article, thus reasons upon this adaptation principle: "If a man breaks a leg, nature instantly adopts extraordinary measures to insure its repair; but are we entitled to infer that she delights in fractured limbs?" If this be argument, there can be no more said upon the subject. Polygamy and polyandry, among mankind, are the rule, not the exception. Broken legs are the exception, not the rule. The comparison of the "learned" reviewer is, therefore, applicable to monogamy, not to polygamy and polyandry.

suppose that, at the time of the advent of Christ, the general Jewish custom of polygamy had fallen into desuetude in consequence of the prohibition by Roman manners, if not by Roman laws. The reverse was the case; the rigid monogamy of the early Italians was disappearing in the presence of a less austere and a more sensuous life. "The almost sacramental Sabine ceremony of the *confarreatio* (offering of bread before the priest and ten witnesses, of which we still retain a relic in our "bride-cake") was rapidly becoming confined to the use of the Pagan priesthood; and the wife was daily ceasing to regard her husband as *amicum, patrem, tutorem* (friend, father, protector); the dignity and privilege of the *materfamilias* (mother) had declined to the position of *uxor tantummodo* (mere wife); the married Antony had openly espoused Cleopatra, and the daily divorce of Maecenas shocked only the stoic Seneca." To this I will add that the old-bachelor system appeared in its entirety among the philosophers and wits—witness one Horatius Flaccus, who might have been a clubman of the present day.

During a missionary dinner at Abeokuta I was somewhat startled by an account of their treatment of polygamic converts. Having accidentally mentioned that a Protestant bishop in South Africa had adopted to advantage the plan of not separating husbands and wives, I was assured that in Yoruba the severe test of sincerity was always made a *sine qua non* before baptism. This naturally induced an inquiry as to what became of the divorcees. "We marry them," said the Rev. Mr. Collmer, "to some bachelor converts." This appeared to me the greatest insult to common sense, the exercise of a power to bind and to loose with a witness; a right to sanctify adultery pure and simple, to do evil that good may come of it, a proceeding which may make any marriage a no-marriage.*

But I was still more astonished to find, when quoting the opinion of Martin Luther, in the case of Philip of Hesse, that several reverend gentlemen had never heard of it, and most when the Rev. Mr. Gollmer, who manifestly made acquaintance with it for the first time, opined that the said Martin Luther had so lately emerged from the darkness of Romanism, that on this point his inner vision was not strong enough to face the light.*

The reverend gentleman's last objection struck me the more forcibly, as it is evident that to the Roman Catholic Church—which when barely adolescent claimed, and still claims in her decrepitude, the right of precedence over the State—we owe, in modern times, the most curious limitation of human liberty ever forced upon mankind. Let us see what the reviewer says on the subject. I will abridge his excellent sketch.

No council, during the first centuries of the Church, denounced polygamy as a sin, but the apostolic limitation

*Martin Luther allowed Philip, Landgrave of Hesse, for political reasons, to intermarry with a second wife, the first being still living. . . . The Reformer, who said, "If Sarah refuses, take Hagar", regarded, like all the early Christians, saints and sinners, marriage as a purely civil rite. He never hesitated, when the object of the union was impeded, to grant letters of divorce, and he notably held that the polygamy practised under the Mosaic dispensation was lawful in modern times. "For my part", he declares, "I confess that I cannot oppose the man who may wish to marry several wives, and that I do not think such plurality contrary to the Holy Scriptures. This is true wisdom. Human liberty has been sufficiently abridged without imagining any further curtailments."

*The lax law makes the polygamic wife a legitimate wife, the missionary declares her illegitimate and not respectable; he degrades her in her own estimate, and he would drive her an outcast from her home. Could ought be more absurd, more wicked?

of the bishop's household was soon applied to the whole ministry and, in the West, penalties were attached to the practice. The Manicheans and Gnostics condemned marriage *in toto,* because it is founded on concupiscence and propagates the work of the devil in confining human souls in the bodies of matter: hence Mani called his elect or perfect—the class above the hearers—men-virgins. This heresy was rebutted, but it seems to have found place in the minds of men. St. Jerome, who is accused by the Reformers of thinking too exclusively of "victuals and virginity," would not undertake to declare a polygamist in mortal sin (*Epistle to Pammachius,* where he writes "I do not condemn polygamists"). St. Augustine (*Against Faustus,* Book 22) is even more precise: "When it was the custom to have more than one wife, it was no crime; now it is a crime, because it is no longer the custom." Polygamy was forbidden throughout the empire by the imperial decrees of A.D. 393, but within thirty years the Emperor Valentinian restored the liberty of marriage, according to the several customs and religions of the inhabitants of the Roman world. Even in the later days the Merovingian kings took as many wives simultaneously as suited their passions or their politics, and "Charlemagne, an eminently Christian emperor, paraded as large a harem as an Oriental sultan would have decorously concealed." Probably, in the presence of such disorders, that development of the doctrine and discipline of the Roman Catholic Church took place which ended in marriage being taken out of the category of personal contracts and, according to the character of the participants, crowned as a sacrament or branded as a sin. In these latter days the claims of polygamy have been wholly neglected. A late work (*La Régéneration du Monde, opuscule dédié aux douze tribus d'Israël,* by M. Joseph de Félicité), contains the following curious sentences: "It is therefore essential that these peoples (the Jews and Moslems) should know that polygamy, which was authorized and practiced until the time of Christ, was revoked by Him (when? where?), and that it was forbidden by Holy Church by the decree of the 24th Session of the Council of Trent which states: 'If any say that it is lawful for Christian men to have several wives, and that it is not forbidden by any law of God, let him be anathema.' " But there is an older and more terrible anathema upon him who takes away from or adds to a word of what was spoken, and perhaps, even the Council of Trent will not be held guiltless.

It is, therefore, among dissidents from the Church of Rome that we must look for assertions touching the lawfulness of polygamy. The advocates are of two classes. The first is of the Casuists—the German Reformers, for instance—who permit the practice in exceptional cases of individual temperament or state necessity, such as might be the subjects of especial dispensation in the Roman Church; the second is of the Moralists, who, without regarding polygamy as an absolute good, still look upon it as a preservative from the miseries and disgraces incident to the illicit intercourse of the sexes in countries where marriage is restricted and men are licentious.* To this class belong the Saxon Lyserus (author of *Polygamia Triumphatrix,* under the name of Theophilus Aletheus), Bishops Berkeley and Burnett—who concludes by saying that "he can see nothing so strong against polygamy as to

*There is nothing more curious in the moral world than to watch the effects of restriction of marriage by increased luxury and expense in England, France, and other so-called civilized lands. Polygamy has been cast out except among the few who can afford to practice an illegal concubinage, and polyandry has now become the last resource of those unable or unwilling to marry.

137

balance the great and visible hazards that hang over so many thousands if it be not allowed"—the Rev. Mr. Madan, who, in his *The Lyphthora,* would give to seduction all the responsibilities of marriage, and the "oblique advocate," poetic Cowper. In 1784, the argument was revived in Russia by the Comte de Rantzow, who asserted that Frederick of Sweden had lately proposed to the states of his kingdom—where bigamy is punished with extreme severity—to permit polygamy, and that the project had been accepted by the two Lower, but rejected by the two Upper Houses of the legislature.

To conclude: I would assure these and other missionaries that had less objection been made to polygamy on their part, the heathen would have found far fewer obstacles to conversion. Those who hold it their duty to save souls, should seriously consider whether they are justified in placing such stumbling blocks upon the path of improvement.

While the diplomatic mission made its way up the Ogun River to Abeokuta, Burton was struck by the absence of feminine modesty:

On the Ogun River we had ample opportunity of forming judgment concerning

The naked Negro panting on the Line.

I have traveled among wild tribes from the North American Indians to the Bhils of Hindustan, but I never saw such an utter absence of what we conventionally term modesty as among these Egbas. The women will stand up and bathe publicly in the river, without a vestige of dress or shame; and the niggerlings are as much clad as the

138

Promutuans and the sons of the Coral Islands. Can this be innocence, as some think? Or is it the mere absence of all ideas of propriety? I confess myself unable to decide.

He was later to recall to what lengths men will go to circumvent the modesty of women. In *The Arabian Nights, vol* IX, in a footnote to the 936th Night, he explains that in Egypt and Syria

. . . a clout hung over the door shows that women are bathing. I have heard, but only heard, that in times and places when eunuchs went in with the women, youths managed by long practice to retract the testicles so as to pass for castratos. It is hard to say what perseverance may not effect in this line . . .

When the party reached Abeokuta, Burton, who had no diplomatic functions to perform, was able to devote his attention to the place and its inhabitants.

There was a vast variety of tattoos and ornaments, rendering them a serious difficulty to strangers. The skin patterns were of every variety, from the diminutive prick to the great gash and the large boil-like lumps. In this country every tribe, sub-tribe, and even family has its blazon, whose infinite diversifications may be compared with the lines and ordinaries of European heraldry. . . . The distinguishing mark of the Egbas is a gridiron of three cuts, or a multiplication of three upon each cheek. Freeborn women have one, two, or three raised lines, thread-like scars from the wrist up the back of the arm, and down the dorsal regions, like long necklaces. They call this "entice my husband". . . . I observed a thing novel to me; the aureola in the women was not infrequently tattooed a dull dark blue, the coloring matter being native antimony, found in Yoruba and on the Niger, and levigated with pepper and natron upon a stone. The jewelry was coral, in necklaces and wristlets, heavy bangles, and anklets of copper, iron, tin, or brass, and various rings upon the thumb, the middle finger, and the toes. . . .

The Abeokutan, when taken at his best, is tall and well-made, "black, but comely." When not so, he is hideously chimpanzeelike. The male figure here, as all the world over, is notably superior, as among the lower mammals, to that of the female. The latter is a system of soft, curved, and rounded lines, graceful, but meaningless and monotonous. The former far excels it in variety of form and in nobility of make, in strength of bone and in suppleness of muscle and sinew. In these lands, where all figures are semi-nude, the exceeding difference between the sexes strikes the eye at once. There will be a score of fine male figures to one female, and there she is, as everywhere else, as inferior as is the Venus de' Medici to the Apollo Belvedere. In Africa also, where the female figure lacks support, it is soon destroyed. The breasts in women are naturally large; after the first child they become pendant and flaccid, and in old age they shrink to mere purses and lappets of skin. It is a curious fact that these withered crones will sometimes suckle children, and that the grandam is used as a wet nurse. In some cases I remarked that, after the fashion of the true Amazons, one breast was well developed, while the other hardly appeared—probably for want of use.*

*Should the reader think it improbable that an aged grandmother might be used as a wet nurse, Burton is ready to suggest that a virgin might likewise be used. In a footnote he writes:

I can hardly, however, rely upon the case quoted by Dr. Clarke, of Sierra Leone, viz., that the stimulus of suckling an orphan monkey caused a lacteal flow from the breasts of a virgin Negress; yet there is no reason for disbelieving the possibility. Embrocations of virgin's milk are not uncommon in the Asiatic and the African pharmacopoeia.

It is almost certain that during this trip to Abeokuta Burton seized the opportunity to cross over into neighboring Dahomey. When discussing Abeokuta's history, and in particular the Dahoman attack that took place in 1851, he manages to elaborate upon the Amazons of the Dahoman army in a way that suggests he had direct knowledge of this curious contingent. He was not impressed by them. "An equal number of British charwomen," he writes, "armed with the British broomstick, would . . . clear them off in a very few hours."

Much nonsense is afloat touching these "Amazons." They are simply, like the Urdubegani of the Deccan and of other Asiatic courts, the slaves of the palace organized as royal property, and weaponed by the late King Gezo— who feared treason from the men. Most of them are women taken in adultery or too shrewish to live with their husbands, who "dash" them to the king, instead of killing them. Once, however, royal slaves they become vestals. They are bound, like female priests of Grewhe, under penalty of death, to chastity and celibacy, and this naturally communicates a certain amount of ferocity to their minds—"horrors" are, as with the eunuch, their substitute for love. Upon this subject I am tempted to quote a few lines from Captain John Adams (p. 74), who says of Dahome: "One of the conditions by which a female is admitted into the order of priesthood, is that of leading a life of celibacy, and renouncing the pleasures of the world; and but few are admitted to enter it at all; for during residence of many months at Grewhe, one ceremony only of this kind was performed, at which I was present.

"There is a striking similarity in the conditions imposed on those poor deluded African women who are admitted into the priesthood, and many of those nuns who in

Catholic Europe are forced to take the veil; only the former are instruments in the hands of fraud and oppression, while the others are too often victims of domestic tyranny and ambition. But the lot of the savage African is far superior to that of the civilized European. For the former, notwithstanding the restraints imposed on her, can enjoy the sweets of personal liberty, and has some scope for the play of her natural affections; where as the latter is shut within the gloomy walls of a prison, where her short life is passed away in vain regret, and in the society of immolated beings who are as melancholy and desponding as herself."

To which we may add, another advantage to the African woman, that her feelings, like those of barbarians and the uncivilized generally, are by no means so highly developed as among Europeans. A scanty diet, a life of toil, and the petty cares of domestic duties, blunt, if they do not destroy, the sexual appetite. She is not even—

> Commanded
> By such poor passion as the maid that milks,
> And does the meanest chares.

Female soldiery, as a rule, is a failure; or rather, like female labor in all departments of industry, it produces a worse article at a cheaper rate. The Amazons, I believe, are no exception.

The modern reader must wonder what Isabel Burton, who was a Roman Catholic, felt about her husband's approval of the comparison between European nuns and African Amazons. But she had other worries, too. On the return journey downriver the diplomatic party stopped once more at Baragu, where they spent a right merry evening. Our hosts were perfectly civil and obliging, and so were our hostesses—rather too much so I could prove, if privileged to whisper in the reader's ear. But what would Mrs. Grundy say?"

What indeed! And what did Isabel Burton say?

7. Dahomey

Burton returned to Fernando Po, to set out almost immediately to explore another portion of his domain, the Cameroons. In February 1862 he was back in his consulate, but in March he was in Gabon. August found him in Benin. December saw him reunited with his wife in England.

On his return to Fernando Po early in 1863 he soon managed to visit the Congo River and Angola. While away on one of his unofficial journeys he must have been surprised to receive a letter from Lord John Russell at the Foreign Office, dated August 20, 1863, appointing him Her Majesty's Commissioner to Dahomey. As Burton wrote later: "Her Majesty's Government had been pleased to choose me as the bearer of a friendly message to King Gelele." However friendly may have been the tone of the message, the transmission of its contents required considerable tact, for the message was an attempt to persuade the King of the importance that Her Majesty's Government attached to the cessation of the slave traffic in Dahomey. Burton's account of this mission was to appear in a

144

book published in 1864, carrying the resounding title: *A Mission to Gelele, King of Dahomey, with Notices of the so-called "Amazons," the grand customs, the yearly customs, the human sacrifices, the present state of the slave trade and the Negro's place in Nature.*

He set out at the end of November, and on December 5th he landed at Ouidah (which he spelled Wydah). A fortnight later he was in Abomey, the capital of Dahomey. On the way there he noted, without surprise but with some slight regret at the missed opportunity for financial gain, the prevalence of phallic worship in the country.

Among all barbarians whose primal want is progeny, we observe a greater or less development of the Phallic worship. In Dahomey it is uncomfortably prominent; every street from Wydah to the capital is adorned with the symbol, and the old ones are not removed. The Dahoman Priapus is a clay figure of any size between a giant and the pygmy, crouched upon the ground as if contemplating its own Attributes. The head is sometimes a wooden block rudely carved, more often dried mud, and the teeth and eyes are supplied by cowries. A huge penis, like the section of a broomstick, rudely carved as the Japanese articles which I have lately been permitted to inspect, projects horizontally from the middle. I could have carried off a donkey's load had I been aware of the rapidly rising value of phallic specimens amongst the collectors of Europe. The Tree of Life is anointed with palm oil, which drips into a pot or a shard placed below it, and the would-be mother of children prays that the great god Legba will make her fertile. There is another Phallic god named "Bo," the guardian of warriors and the protector of markets. Female Legbas are rare, about one to a dozen males. They are, if possible, more hideous and gorillalike than those of the other sex; their breasts resemble the halves of German sausages, and the external labia, which are adored by being anointed with oil, are painfully developed.

Burton recognized that phallic worship was "one of those peculiarities of Dahoman race, which, in the usual phrase, are 'unfit for the drawing-room table.' " He did not, therefore, include it in his book, but published the information in a paper entitled "Notes on the Dahoman" in *Memoirs Read Before the Anthropological Society of London* (Vol. 1, 1865, pp. 308-321). That the "peculiarities" were also unfit for the drawing room tables of the 1920's is suggested by the fact that it was an edited version of this paper that appeared in *Selected Papers on Anthropology, Travel and Exploration by Sir Richard Burton,* Edited by N. M. Penzer (1924).

The mission to Abomey presented Burton with the opportunity of learning the facts about the Amazons, the women soldiers of King Gelele's army. In his book, *A Mission to Gelele,* he devoted a chapter to them, entitled "Of the So-called Amazons and the Dahoman Army," in which he ranged characteristically well beyond the ranks of that unusual force:

A chronic exaggeration touching upon the miscalled "Amazons" (the word is probably some barbarian term Grecised). It has three popular derivations—the Scythian, Amm Azzon, which the Greeks interpreted, "without breasts"; ἄνευ μὰζον, without a breast (the right), mythically believed to have been removed for the better use of the bow; thirdly, ἀμαζωσας, or women living together, has of late years prevailed in England. Mr. Duncan found it "certainly a surprising sight in an uncivilized country." Commander Forbes, who drew, as artists say, "from feeling," was the first to color the melodramatic picture with a

146

"sensation" and picturesqueness, a sentiment and a wild romance, in which the real object is wholly wanting. He begins his account with the untraveled statement that "there is not a more extraordinary army in the world than that of the military nation of Dahomey."

The origin of the somewhat exceptional organization is, as I have said, the masculine *physique* of the women, enabling them to compete with men in enduring toil, hardships and privations. I have remarked this corporeal equality of the sexes in the Grand Bonny and the "Oil Rivers" of the Biafran Bight, where the female harshness of feature and robustness of form rival the masculine: and writers upon Siam have made the same observation.

Bosman (1700) allows the kinglet of Whydah 4,000 to 5,000 wives, who, besides laboring in the fields, were used to execute the royal sentences.* The monarch of Yoruba, according to Clapperton, could boast that his wives, of whom some composed his bodyguard, would, linked hand in hand, reach clean across his kingdom. The late King Gezo used to boast that he had organized the Mi-no (a Dahoman term for the soldieresses); but the *History*** depicts them before he was born. The Europeans who visited Agaja (1708-1730), found the Dahoman Court much as it is in the present day. . . . The same volume also informs us that the warlike monarch, when his force had been reduced by the "Eyeos," "armed a great number of the women like soldiers, having their proper officers,

---

*But the King of Dahomey, it must be observed, distinguishes between his wives and his soldieresses. At court the former are unarmed, the latter carry weapons and do not commonly expect his particular attentions.

**The History of Dahomey, an Island Kingdom of Africa; compiled from Authentic Memoirs; with an Introduction and Notes, by Archibald Dalzel, 1763.

and furnished like regular troops with drums, colors and umbrellas, making at a distance a very formidable appearance." With these, in about A.D. 1728, he attacked and defeated the combined host of the Whydahs and Popos, and since that time the Amazons have ever been a power in the empire.

Doubtless Gezo, one of the most successful among the Dahoman monarchs, regarded the feminine force with a favoring eye. He depended upon it to check the turbulence and treachery of his subjects, and to ensure his own safety, for

Who causes terror is himself the more subject to fear; a fate befitting tyrants.

He may have also wished to cause rivalry, by the example of what is in most cases illogically termed the "weaker sex."* Perhaps, like the old-school Anglo-Indian nabob, he may have preferred the maid to the manservant.

*Because we make it so. The feminidae, like the females of the equidae, show little corporeal inferiority to the males, and the best proof is, that among the tribes living in the so-called State of Nature, women are generally the only laborers. We may etiolate them, as in New England, or we may expand them, by beef and beer, to grenadiers, as in olden England and in the north of Europe. To the present day the woman of the Scotch fishing islands is the man of the family, who does not marry till she can support what she produces; and the times are not long past since she was, among the Southrons, a barber, a mason and a day laborer.

It appears to me that in England there is a revival of the feminine industries; and when it is asked, "What shall we do with our old maids?" I would reply that many might be enlisted. When Mr. Duncan was asked by the King of Dahomey if the same number of Englishwomen would equal the Ama-

Gezo ordered every Dahoman of note in the kingdom to present his daughters, of whom the most promising were chosen, and he kept the corps clear of the servile and the captive. Gelele, his son, causes every girl to be brought to him before marriage, and if she pleases, he retains her in the palace: the only subjects exempt from this rule are the old English and French slaves at Whydah. These girls, being royal wives, cannot be touched without danger of death, they never leave their quarters unless preceded by a bell to drive men from the road, and all have slaves who act as spies. The sexes meet on the march and in the field: at parades, as has been shown, they are separated by the typical bamboo. A peculiar fetish, placed by the priests at the Agbo-dewe gate of the royal abode, induces, by reason of the purity of the place, certain pregnancy in the soldieress that sins. Instances have been known where conscience has made the offender coward enough to sicken, to confess, and to doom her

zons, he, of course, answered *no;* we had no female soldiers in England, but we had women who, individually and voluntarily, had equally distinguished themselves. Such feminine troops would serve well in garrison, and eventually in the field. The Medea of Euripides preferred the risks of spear and shield among men to a single casualty after the manner of women. The warlike instinct, as the annals of the four quarters of the globe prove, is easily bred in the opposite sex. A sprinkling of youth and beauty among the European Amazons would make campaigning a pleasure to us; and the measures may be taken into consideration when our newfangled rage for neutrality shall be succeeded by more honorable and less "respectable" sentiments; and when the model Englishman shall be something better than a warm man of business, with a good ledger, and "the dean's daughter" to wife.

paramour, if not herself, to a cruel death. They have also a "pundonor." Like

> That Mary Ambree
> Who marched so free,

many an Amazon captured at Abeokuta has refused to become a wife till the captor, weary of opposition, has killed the shrewish girl as a useless animal.*

Of Gelele's Amazons about two-thirds are said to be maidens, a peculiar body in Africa, where, though 11,000 may have been buried at Cologne, no one expects to find the unsullied virgin, much less the old maid. The remaining third has been married. That an element of desperation might not be wanting, women taken in adultery and liable to death are dashed to the king and duly enlisted. Besides these criminals, the Xanthippes, who make men's eyes yellow, are very properly put into the army, and Africa is well stocked with the noble army of martyrs that begins not with Socrates, and that ends not with Mr. Thomas Sayers.

It is evident that such an organization presents nought of novelty: the systematic organization is more logical and less harmful than the volunteer Furies who, as Abolitionists, urge men to ruin and death. The soldieress, at least, joins in the danger, this thing does not. David flying from Absalom left ten of his concubines to guard his palace at Jerusalem. The Greeks probably derived their Amazonian

---

*Though opportunity, which makes the thief, is decidedly deficient, there have been, there are, and there ever will be occasional scandals. As a rule, these fighting celibates prefer the perverted pleasure of the schoolmen, and the peculiarities of the Tenth Muse.

myth from exaggerated reports of the strength and valor of the Caucasian women. With respect to the visit of Thalestris, who desired issue by the conqueror of Asia (which Arrian has exploded), it is no more than what many a Bedawiyah will solicit from the traveler who in a fair fight beats off her husband and brother. Among the Homerites of South Arabia it was a law for wives to revenge in battle the deaths of their husbands, and mothers their sons. The Suliote women rivaled the men in defending their homes against Osmanli invaders. The Damot or Abyssinian Amazons of Alvarez (1520) would not allow their spouses to fight, as the Jivaro helpmates of southern America administer caudle to the sex that requires it the least. The native princes of India, especially those of Hyderabad in the Deccan, for centuries maintained a female guard of Urdu-begani, whose courage and devotion were remarkable. Bodies of European fighting women were found in the celebrated "Female Crusade," organized in 1147 by order of St. Bernard. Temba-Ndumba, among the Jagas of southern intertropical Africa, according to old travelers, made her subjects rear and teach their female children war, but she was probably mad.*

The Tawarik women rank with men like the women of Christianity, and transmit nobility to their children. Denham found the Fellatah wives fighting like males. According to Mr. Thompson (1823), the Mantati host that

*In *Savage Africa,* a book which has before been quoted, we read that this amiable Ethiopian pounded in a mortar her own male child to make an invulnerable ointment; that she resolved to turn the world into a desert, and did her best: and, finally, that waxing worse with years, she took a lover to her arms by night and dined off him next day. Of course this black Scourge of God was poisoned.

151

attacked old "Lattaku" was led by a ferocious giantess with one eye. M. D'Arnaud (1840) informs us that the King of Behr, on the Upper Nile, was guarded by a battalion of spear women, and that his male ministers never enter the palace, except when required to perform the melancholy duty of strangling their master. At present the Tien-Wang or Heavenly King of the Tae-pings, has 1,000 she-soldiers.

Sporadic heroines, like Tomrys and Penthesilea of the Axe, are found in every clime and in all ages, from Semiramis to the artilleryman's wife of Saragossa. Such were Judith and Candace; Kaulah the sister of Derar, and her friend Oserrah; the wife of Aban Ibn Saib; Prefect Gregory's daughter; Joan of Arc: Margaret of Anjou; Black Agnes; Jeanne Hachette; Begum Sombre; Kara Fatimah; Panna Maryan, and many

> A bold virago stout and tall,
> As Joan of Arc, or English Moll

—charmers far too numerous to specify. Many a fair form was found stark on the field of Waterloo. During the late Indian mutiny the Ranis were, as a rule, more manly than the Rajahs. And the present Anglo-American states and Poland show women who, despite every discouragement, still prefer the military profession to all others.*

*On the other hand, the notorious Queen Zinga, or Jinga of Angola, as she is called by the old travelers, daughter of the king who died in 1640, kept, we are told, about her court, fifty or sixty young men for amatory purposes, dressed and named like women, while she assumed the male dress and name; a touching tribute to the superiority of masculine human nature in the mind of the feminine. The Court of Loango

The regimen in which these women are compelled to live increases their ferocity in fight. It is the essence of training every animal, from a gamecock to a pugilist, and a married she-soldier would be useful only as the mother of men. Commander Forbes thus explains the action of forced celibacy: "The extreme exercise of one passion will generally obliterate the very sense of the others; the Amazons, while indulging in the excitement of the most fearful cruelties, forget the other desires of our fallen nature." But all the passions are sisters. I believe that bloodshed causes these women to remember, not to forget, LOVE; at the same time that it gratifies the less barbarous, but, with barbarians, equally animal feeling. Seeing the host of women who find a morbid pleasure in attending the maimed and dying. I must think that it is a tribute paid to sexuality by those who object to the ordinary means. Of course they are savage as wounded gorillas, more cruel by far than their brethren in arms.

> For men at most differ as heaven and earth;
> But women, worst and best, as heaven and hell.

Apart from phallic worship, there were other aspects of Dahoman life which Burton considered too anthropological for the general reader and which he described in his *Notes on the Dahoman* referred to above:

The Dahoman is essentially a polygynist; and the *His-*

offered a third anomaly, truly typical of the childish African brain. The Macouda, a female officer of high rank, cohabited with any man of her choice; the issue was accounted royal blood; and if her concubators were unfaithful, death was their penalty. A touching tribute to the superiority of the female in those regions.

tory [by Dalzell] is still correct in asserting "the Dahoman women do not admit the embraces of their husbands
during pregnancy, nor at the time of suckling, which
continues two or three years, nor during menstruation,
when they retire to a part of the town allotted to their
reception. The prostitutes in this country are licensed by
royal authority, are also obliged to confine themselves to a
particular district, and are subject to an annual tax." The
latter class, called *ko'si* (twenty-wife), because the honorarium was twenty cowries, is supplied from the palace;
and the peculiar male and female system which pervades
the court rendering eunuchesses necessary as well as eunuchs, demands *Hetaerae* for the women as well as for the
male fighters. I was hardly prepared for this amount of
cynicism amongst mere barbarians; although in that won-
derful book, *The Arabian Nights,* which has been degrad-
ed by Europe into mere fairy tales, the lover is always
jealous, not of his own, but of the opposite sex.

Another great peculiarity in Dahomey is as follows:
almost all the world over, where man is circumcised, the
woman is subjected either, as in Egypt, to mutilation of
the clitoris, performed in early infancy when that part is
prominent, or as in the Somal and the Upper Nilotic
tribes, described by M. Werne (*Reise zur Entdeckung der
Quellen des Weissen Nil*) [N. M. Penzer has pointed out
that it was in *Reise durch Sennar nach Manders, Nasub,
Cheli, im Lande zwischen dem blauen Nil und dem At-
bara* that Werne described clitorectomy of the Niletic
tribes] to mutilation combined with excision of the nymphae and fibulation, the wounded surfaces being roughly
stitched together. The reason of such mutilation is evident.
Removal of the prepuce blunts the sensitiveness of the
glans penis, and protracts the act of Venus, which Africans and Asiatics ever strive, even by charms and medi-

154

cines, to lengthen. The clitoris, called by old authors the well and fountainhead of sexual pleasure, must be reduced to a similar condition, or the too frequent recurrence of the venereal orgasm would injure the health of the woman. This is the case in the Old Calabar River of the Biafran Bight; in Dahomey it is the reverse.

Adagbwiba, or circumcision, which in parts of West Africa, the Gold Coast for instance, appears sporadic, is universally practiced in Dahomey. During the days of the *History* (Introduction, p. xviii) the time of submitting to the rite was left to the boys themselves, and their caresses were not admitted by the women as long as they remained in the natural state. At present, circumcision is undergone in Whyda (now spelled Ouidah) and about the seaboard at the age of twelve to sixteen; in the interior it is often delayed till the youth is twenty years old, when it becomes cruel and sometimes dangerous. It is apparently not a religious ceremony: a lay practitioner, and not the fetishman, being the performer. The patient sits over a small hole dug in the ground. The operator draws out the prepuce, which, as among Africans generally, is long and fleshy, and removes the blood from it by manipulation. He then inserts under the prepuce the forefinger of the left hand, and wetting with saliva a splint or a bit of straw, marks the circle which is to be removed. Two cuts with a sharp razor, one above the other below, conclude the operation. This would argue an origin unconnected with the Jewish and with the Moslem forms, which also vary; among circumcising peoples, however, the rite is everywhere differently performed. The favorite styptic is heated sand thrown on the wound, which is washed every third day with simples boiled in water. The drink is ginger and warm water, the food is ginger soup, but anything may be eaten except pork.

155

"A certain operation peculiar to this country," says the *History*, "is likewise performed upon the woman," and this the footnote thus explains: "Namely, the artificial lengthening of the labia until they are very like the teats of a she-goat." The parts in question, locally called *Tu*, must, from the earliest years, be manipulated by professional old women, as is the bosom among the embryo prostitutes of China. If this be neglected, the lady friends will deride and denigrate the mother, declaring that she has neglected her child's education, and the juniors will laugh at the daughter as a coward who would not prepare herself for marriage. The sole possible advantage to be derived from this strange practice is the prevention of rape, but the men are said to enjoy handling the long projections, whose vivid slatey hue suggests the idea of a turkey-cock's caruncle. It is properly said, "There can be no pleasurable Venus without 'Tu.'" I find the custom among the cognate tribes of Grand Popo, but not in any other part of the west African coast.

The anthropologist in Burton found the practice of male and female circumcision, and the great variety of ways in which the operation was performed, of absorbing interest. A long footnote to "The Tale of the Damsel Tohfat al 'Kulub" in *The Arabian Nights* (Supplemental vol. II, pp. 90-93) shows how wide had been his observation and reading on this particular subject:

I here propose to consider at some length this curious custom (circumcision) which has prevailed among so many widely separated races. Its object has been noted (vol. v, p. 209), viz., to diminish the sensitivity of the glans, no longer lubricated with prostatic lymph; this the part is hardened against injury and disease and its work in coition is prolonged. On the other hand "the foreskin increases (the woman's) pleasure in sexual intercourse, and therefore women prefer intercourse with uncircumcised men rather than with Turks and Jews," says Dimerbroeck (*Anatomie*). I vehemently doubt the fact. Circumcision was doubtless practised from ages immemorial by the people of Central Africa, and Welcker found traces of it in a mummy of the sixteenth century B.C. The Jews borrowed it from the Egyptian priesthood and made it a manner of sacrament, "uncircumcised" being="unbaptized," that is, barbarian, heretic; it was a seal of reconciliation, a sign of alliance between the Creator and the Chosen People, a token of nationality imposed upon the body politic. Thus it became a cruel and odious protestation against the brotherhood of man, and the cosmopolitan Roman derided the circumcised male and female. The Jews also used the term figuratively as the "circumcision of fruits" (Lex. xix, 23), and of the heart (Deut., x, 16); and the old law gives copious historical details of its origin and continuance. Abraham first amputated his horny foreskin at the age of ninety-nine, and did the same for his son and household (Gen., xvii, 24-27). The rite caused a separation between Moses and his wife (Exod., iv, 25). It was suspended during the Desert Wanderings and was resumed by Joshua (v, 3-7) who cut off two tons weight of prepuces. The latter became, like the scalps of the Scythians and North American "Indians," trophies of victory; Saul promised his daughter Michol to David for a dowry of one hundred, and the son-in-law brought a double tale.

Among the early Christians opinions concerning the rite differed. Although the Founder of Christianity was circumcised, St. Paul, who aimed at a cosmopolitan faith, discouraged it in the physical phase. St. Augustine still sustained that the rite removed original sin despite the Fathers who preceded and followed him: Justus, Tertul-

157

lian, Ambrose, and others. But it gradually lapsed into desuetude and was preserved only in the outlying regions. Paulus Jovius and Munster found it practiced in Abyssinia, but as a mark of nobility confined to the descendants of "Nicaules, queen of Sheba." The Abyssinians still follow the Jews in performing the rite within eight days after the birth and baptize boys after forty and girls after eighty days. When a circumcised man became a Jew he was bled before three witnesses at the place where the prepuce had been cut off, and this was called the "Blood of Alliance." Apostate Jews effaced the sign of circumcision: so in 1 Macc., i, 16, they made themselves uncircumcised and forsook the covenant. Thus making prepuces was called by the Hebrews Meshookim=recutitis, and there is an allusion to it in 1 Cor., vii, 18, 19, μὴ ἐπισπασθαι (Farrar, Paul, ii., 70). St. Jerome and others deny the possibility; but Mirabeau (*Akropodie*) relates how Father Conning by liniments of oil, suspending weights, and wearing the virga in a box gained in 43 days 7¼ lines [one line= 1/12 inch.] The process is still practiced by Armenians and other Christians who, compelled to Islamise, wish to return to Christianity. I cannot however find a similar artifice applied to a circumcised clitoris. The simplest form of circumcision is mere amputation of the prepuce and I have noted (vol. v, 209) the difference between the Moslem and the Jewish rite, the latter according to some being supposed to heal in kindlier way. But the varieties of circumcision are immense. Probably none is more terrible than that practiced in the province Al-Asír, the old Ophir, lying south of Al-Hijáz, where it is called Salkh, lit.=scarification. The patient, usually from ten to twelve years old, is placed upon raised ground holding in right hand a spear, whose heel rests upon his foot and whose point shows every tremor of the nerves. The tribe stands about him to pass judgment on his fortitude, and the barber performs the operation with the Jumbiyak-dagger, sharp as a razor. First he makes a shallow cut, severing only the skin across the belly immediately below the navel, and similar incisions down each groin; then he tears off the epidermis from the cuts downwards and flays the testicles and penis, ending with amputation of the foreskin. Meanwhile the spear must not tremble and in some clans the lad holds a dagger over the back of the stooping barber, crying, "Cut and fear not!" When the ordeal is over, he exclaims "Allaho Akbar!" and attempts to walk toward the tents, soon falling for pain and nervous exhaustion, but the more steps he takes the more applause he gains. He is dieted with camel's milk, the wound is treated with salt and turmeric, and the chances in his favor are about ten to one. No body-pile or pubic hair ever grows upon the excoriated part which preserves through life a livid ashen hue. While Mohammed Ali Pasha occupied the province he forbade "scarification" under pain of impalement, but it was resumed the moment he left Al-Asir. In Africa not only is circumcision indigenous, the operation varies more or less in the different tribes. In Dahome it is termed Adda-gwibi, and is performed between the twelfth and twentieth years. The rough operation is made peculiar by a double cut above and below, the prepuce being treated in the Moslem, not the Jewish fashion. Heated sand is applied as a styptic and the patient is dieted with ginger-soup and warm drinks of ginger-water, pork being especially forbidden. The Fantis of the Gold Coast circumcise in sacred places, e.g., at Accra on a Fetish rock rising from the sea. The peoples of Sennaar, Taka, Masawwah and the adjacent regions follow the Abyssinian custom. The barbarous Bissagos and Fellups of northwestern Guinea make cuts on the prepuce without amputating it; while the Baquens and Papels circumcise like Moslems. The blacks of Loango are all circumcised, otherwise they would be rejected by the women. The Bantu or Caffre tribes are circumcised between the ages of fifteen and eighteen; the "Fetish boys," as we call them, are chalked white and wear only grass belts; they live outside the villages in special houses under an old "medicine-man," who teaches them not only virile arts but also to rob and fight. The "man-making" may last five months and ends in fetes and dances; the patients are washed in the river, they burn down their quarters, take new names, and become adults, donning a kind of straw thimble over the prepuce. In Madagascar three several cuts are made, causing much suffering to the children; and the nearest male relative swallows the prepuce. The Polynesians circumcise when childhood ends and thus consecrate the fecunding organs to the Deity. In Tahiti the operation is performed by the priest, and in Tonga only the priest is exempt. The Maoris on the other hand fasten the prepuce over the glans, and women of the Marquesas Islands have shown great cruelty to shipwrecked sailors who expose the glans. Almost all the known Australian tribes circumcise after some fashion: Bennet supposes the rite to have been borrowed from the Malays, while Gason enumerates the "Kurrawellie wonkauna" among the five mutilations of puberty. Leichhardt found circumcision about the Gulf of Carpentaria and in the river valleys of the Robinson and Macarthur: others observed it on the southern coast and among the savages of Perth, where it is noticed by Salvado. James Dawson tells us boys are circumcised, etc., in western Victoria. Brough Smyth, who supposes the object is to limit population (?), describes on the western coast and in Central Australia the "Corroberee" dance and the operation performed with a quartz

160

flake. Teichelmann details the rite in southern Australia where the assistants—all men, women and children being driven away—form a manner of "human altar" upon which the youth is laid for circumcision. He then receives the normal two names, public and secret, and is initiated into the mysteries proper for men. The Australians also for Malthusian reasons produce an artificial hypospadias, while the Karens of New Guinea only split the prepuce longitudinally (*Cosmos,* p. 369, October 1876): the indigens of Port Lincoln on the west coast split the virga: the lower part of the penis is split to the urethra between the ages of twelve and fourteen, says E. J. Eyre in 1845. Missionary Schürmann declares they open the urethra. Gason describes in the Dieyerie tribe the operation "Kulpi" which is performed when the beard is long enough for tying. The member is placed upon a slab of tree bark, the urethra is incised with a quartz flake mounted in a gum handle and a splinter of bark is inserted to keep the cut open. These men may appear naked before women who expect others to clothe themselves. Miklucho Maclay calls it "Mika" in central Australia; he was told by a squatter that of three hundred men only three or four had the member intact in order to get children, and that in one tribe the female births greatly outnumbered the male. Those mutilated also marry: when making water they sit like women slightly raising the penis, this in coition becomes flat and broad and the semen does not enter the matrix. The explorer believes that the deed of kind is more quickly done(?). Circumcision was also known to the New World. Herrera relates that certain Mexicans cut off the ears and prepuce of the newly born child, causing many to die. The Jews did not adopt the female circumcision of Egypt described by Huet on Origen: "Circumcision of women by cutting the nymphae, or clitoris, which grows so luxuriantly in women in Southern countries that is must be pruned back by the knife." Here we have the normal confusion between excision of the nymphae (usually for fibulation) and circumcision of the clitoris. Bruce notices this clitorectomy among the Abyssinians. Werne describes the excision on the Upper White Nile and I have noted the complicated operation among the Somali tribes. Girls in Dahomey are circumcised by ancient midwives, and a woman in the natural state would be derided by everyone. The Australians cut out the clitoris, and as I have noted elsewhere extirpate the ovary for Malthusian purposes (*Journ. Anthrop. Inst.,* vol. viii of 1884).

The royal wives of Dahomey, like the women of Eastern harems, had to be guarded if the king were to avoid sharing them with the more adventurous of his subjects. For this purpose it no doubt seemed appropriate to use eunuchs, who after all had been used in this way for many hundreds of years, often achieving positions of great influence. Surprisingly, Burton was unable to obtain much information about Dahoman eunuchs, who shared with the women they guarded the title of "royal wives." He writes:

As a rule the Dahoman eunuch still marries, and I have heard of cases similar to the one quoted in Dalzel's *History,* when relating the end of the rebel eunuch "Tanga": "To his wives he appeared not the rigid jailer, nor the tyrannic usurper of their affections, but the generous arbiter of their liveliest pleasures. Hence they could not but be charmed with a freedom which no other seraglio enjoyed, and [all devoted themselves to death] they would not survive that felicity and protection which was to terminate with the existence of their master and their lover, whose ruin seemed inevitable." It is difficult to obtain information in Dahomey concerning eunuchs, who are special slaves of the king and bear the dignified title of royal wives. The operation is performed in the palaces, by evulsion of the testicles, and is often fatal, especially when deferred till the age of twenty. Throughout Yoruba these neutrals are found at the different courts, and the practice may have migrated from the East.

This lack of information must have been galling to Burton who, as an anthropologist, was deeply interested in the whole subject of eunuchry. The reader will no doubt be more surprised than Burton appears to have been by the fact that "the Dahoman eunuch marries," and one can only suppose that it was prior to his Dahoman mission that he had had an opportunity of conversing with a eunuch's wife. In a footnote to the "375th Night" (*Arabian Nights,* vol. v, p. 46) he returns to this sad conjunction of half-man and wife:

There are many ways of making the castrato; in some only the penis is removed, in others the testes are bruised or cut off; but in all cases the animal passion remains, for in man, unlike other animals, the fount of sexual pleasure is the brain. The story of Abelard proves this. Juvenal derided the idea of married eunuchs and yet almost all these neutrals have wives with whom they practice the manifold *plaisirs de la petite oie* (masturbation, tribadism, irrumation, tête-bêche, feuille-de-rose, etc.) till they induce the venereal orgasm. Such was the account once given to me by a eunuch's wife; and I need hardly say that she, like her confrère was to be pitied. At the critical moment she held up a little pillow for her husband to bite who otherwise would have torn her cheeks or breasts.

163

This cruel mutilation was not a subject for the general reader. It would surely have interested the Anthropological Society of London, yet Burton published no paper on it in the Journal. One must assume, then, that, having collected during his travels a number of miscellaneous and disjointed notes on eunuchry, it was not until later that he was able to read round the subject and arrange his information with the care that he had given to pederasty and to circumcision. The full results of his observations and reading appeared in *The Arabian Nights* (Supplemental vol. 1, p. 70) in a major footnote to "The Story of the Merchant who Lost his Luck."

"Eunuch," etymologically meaning chamberlain (belonging to the bed chamber), a bedchamber-servant or slave, was presently confined to castrated men found useful for special purposes, like gelded horses, hounds, and cockerels turned to capons. Some writers hold that the creation of the semivir or apocopus began as a punishment in Egypt and elsewhere; and so under the Romans amputation of the "peccant part" was frequent: others trace the Greek "invalid," i.e., impotent man, to marital jealousy, and not a few to the wife who wished to use the sexless for hard work in the house without danger to slave girls. The origin of the mutilation is referred by Ammianus Marcellinus (lib. iv., chap. 17), and the classics generally, to Semiramis, an "ancient queen" of decidedly doubtful epoch, who thus prevented the propagation of weaklings. But in Genesis (xxxvii, 36, xxxix, 1, margin) we find Potiphar termed a "Sarim" (castrato), an attenuating circumstance for Mrs. P., who "cast her eyes upon Joseph; and she said, lie with me." Herodotus (III, chap. 48) tells us that Periander, tyrant of Corinth, sent three hundred Corcyrean boys to Alyattes for castration ἐπὶ ἥτ ἐχτομῆ and that

Panionios of Chios sold caponized lads for high prices (viii, 105): he notices (viii, 104 and other places) that eunuchs "of the Sun, of the Heaven, of the hand of God," were looked upon as honorable men among the Persians whom Stephanus and Brissonius charge with having invented the name (Dabistan i, 171). Ctesias also declares that the Persian kings were under the influence of eunuchs. In the debauched ages of Rome the women found a new use for these effeminates, who had lost only the testes or testiculi=the witnesses (of generative force): it is noticed by Juvenal (i. 22; ii, 365-379; vi, 366)

. . . Some there are who always delight in the kisses of smooth eunuchs.

So Martial,

Gallia wants to copulate but not to bear children.

And Mirabeau knew (see Kadísah) "they bite and caress their women ceaselessly and with refinement." (Compare my vol. ii, 90; v, 40.) The men also used them as catamites (Horace i, 0d. xxxvii):

With a crowd of vile creatures defiled by that disease (i.e., castration).

In religion the natural or artificial eunuch was held ill-omened, and not permitted to become a priest (Seneca Controv. ii, 4), a practice perpetuated in the various Christian churches. The manufacture was forbidden, to the satisfaction of Martial, by Domitian, whose edict Nero confirmed; and was restored by the Byzantine empire, which advanced eunuchs, like Eutropius and Narses, to the highest dignitaries of the realm. The cruel custom to the eternal disgrace of mediaeval Christianity was revived in Rome for providing the choirs in the Sistine Chapel and elsewhere with boys' voices. Isaiah mentions the custom (lvi, 3-6). Mohammed, who notices in the Koran (xxiv, 31), "such men as attend women and have no need of women", i.e. "have no natural force," expressly forbade (iv, 18), "changing Allah's creatures," referring, say the commentators, to superstitious ear-cropping of cattle, tattooing, teeth-sharpening, sodomy, tribadism, and slave-gelding. . . . Yet the Harem perpetuated the practice throughout Al-Islam and African jealousy made a gross abuse of it. To quote no other instance, the Sultan of Dár-For had a thousand eunuchs under a Malik or king, and all the chief offices of the empire, such as Ab (father) and Báb (door), were monopolized by these neutrals. The center of supply was the Upper Nile, where the operation was found dangerous after the age of fifteen, and when badly performed only one in four survived. For this reason, during the last century the Coptic monks of Girgah and Zawy al-Dayr, near Assiout, engaged in this scandalous traffic, and declared that it was philanthropic to operate scientifically (Prof. Panuri and many others). Eunuchs are now made in the Sudan, Nubia, Abyssinia, Kordofan, and Dar-For, especially the Messalmiyah district: one of the towns was called "Tawashah" (eunuchry) from the traffic there conducted by Fakuha or religious teachers. Many are supplied by the district between Majarah (Majarash?) and the port Masawwah; there are also depots at Mbadr, near Tajurrah-harbour, where Yusuf Bey, Governor in 1880, caponized some forty boys, including the brother of a hostile African chief: here also the well-known Abu Bakr was scandalously active. It is calculated that not less than eight thousand of these unfortunates are annually exported to Arabia, Egypt, and Turkey. Article IV of the Anglo-Egyptian Convention punishes the offense with death, and no one would object to hanging the murderer under whose mutilating razor a boy dies. Yet this, like most of our modern "improvements" in Egypt, is a mere empty threat. The crime is committed under our very eyes, but we will not see it.

The Romans numbered three kinds of eunuchs: 1. Castrati, clean-shaved, from Gr. Cestros; 2. Spadones, from Späo when the testicles are torn out, not from "Spada," a town of Persia; and 3. Thlibii, from $\theta_\lambda i\beta\omega$ to press, squeeze, when the testicles are bruised, etc. In the East also, as I have stated (v. 46), eunuchs are of three kinds: 1. Sandali, or the clean-shaved, the classical apocopus. The parts are swept off by a single cut of a razor, a tube (tin or wooden) is set in the urethra, the wound is cauterized with boiling oil, and the patient is planted in a fresh dunghill. His diet is milk; and if under puberty, he often survives. This is the *eunuque aqueduc,* who must pass his water through a tube. 2. The eunuch whose penis is removed: he retains all the powers of copulation and procreation without the wherewithal; and this, since the discovery of rubber, has often been supplied. 3. The eunuch, or classical Thlibias and Semivir, who has been rendered sexless by removing the testicles (as the priests of Cybele were castrated with a stone knife), or by bruising (the Greek Thlásias), twisting, searing, or bandaging them. A more humane process has lately been introduced: a horse hair is tied around the neck of the scrotum and tightened by slow degrees till the circulation of the part stops and the bag drops off without pain. This has been adopted in sundry Indian regiments of Irregular Cavalry, and it succeeded admirably: the animals rarely required a day's rest. The practice was known to the ancients. See notes on

167

Kadisah in Mirabeau. The female eunuch was invented by the Lydians, according to their historian Xanthus. Zachias (Quaest. medico-legal) declares that the process was one of infibulation or simple sewing up the vulva; but modern experience has suggested an operation like the "spaying" of bitches, or mutilation of the womb, in modern euphemism "baby-house." Dr. Robert (*Journey from Delhi to Bombay, Müller's Archiv. 1843*) speaks of a eunuched woman who after ovariotomy had no breasts, no pubes, no rotundities, and no desires. The Australians practice exsection of the ovaries systematically to make women barren. Miklucho Maclay learned from the traveler Retsch that about Lake Parapitshurie men's urethras were split, and the girls were spayed: the latter showing two scars in the groin. They have flat bosoms, but feminine forms, and are slightly bearded; they mix with the men, whom they satisfy mechanically, but without enjoyment (?). MacGillivray, of the "Rattlesnake," saw near Cape York a woman with these scars: she was a surdo-mute, and had probably been spayed to prevent increase. The old Scandinavians, from Norway to Iceland, systematically gelded "sturdy vagrants," in order that they might not beget bastards. The Hottentots before marriage used to cut off the left testicle, meaning by such semi-castration to prevent the begetting of twins. This curious custom, mentioned by the Jesuit Tochard, Boeving, and Kolbe, is now apparently obsolete—at least, the traveler Fritsch did not find it.

Burton had been sent to Dahomey on an official mission. He had gone, not to collect anthropological data, but to persuade the king to cease trading in slaves. From this point of view the mission was a total failure: Gelele could see no reason for bringing the slave trade to an end.

The Commissioner was back on Fernando Po in February, and in August he returned to England for leave.

Thanks to his wife's strenuous efforts, he would not return to Fernando Po: his consulship in the Bight of Biafra had finished.

8. Brazil

Richard Burton, the Great Arabian scholar and linguist, was now appointed to a post that was even farther away from Arabia than the malarial island of Fernando Po, but at least Isabel could go with him. The appointment was the consulship at Santos in Brazil.

The Burtons set out on May 10, 1865. Richard was now aged forty-four, Isabel was thirty-four. Burton was in no hurry to get to his post and decided to see Portugal on the way. The couple spent two months there. When Burton finally left, the ship in which he was sailing called at St. Vincent, Cape Verde Islands, for coal. One result of this brief visit was a letter which Burton sent to the secretary of the Anthropological Society of London and which was published in the society's journal:

Having been asked to commit to paper any anthropological curiosities which met my sight while traveling about the Far West, I send you a few observations made by me at St. Vincent, Cape Verde Islands.

At Novo Mindello, capital town of St. Vincent

(Azores), I was allowed to inspect one of these malformations which go by the name of hermaphrodites. It is considered a boy, and is the son of Serafinis Federigo di Ramos, a guard in the customhouse, and his wife Catharina, who are first cousins. The only other issue is a girl, a specimen of modified albinism, the skin being white and freckled and the hair colorless, while the eyes show no trace of pink.

Antonio de Ramos, as the malformation is called, will be eight years of age in September 1865. He has at present twenty-four teeth. His height is four feet, four inches, his girth under the armpits two feet, four inches, and round the haunches two feet three inches; of womanly size. His hips would project beyond the oval that contains his shoulders; in boys we should expect the contrary. His face is rather that of a boy than a girl. He has decided hemiplegia of the left side, the leg being, however, less affected than the arm, and he has a weak and sickly look, which does not promise longevity.

The penis is distinctly formed, about an inch and a quarter long, and proportionately thick, though not of the large African's size; the naked glans looks as if naturally circumcised. The orifice, instead of being at the top, is under the virga, thus constituting a clear case of hypospadias. The parents declare that he micturates from both organs, but less from the masculine. The urine, therefore, would pass through the frenum. No sign of testicles could be seen or felt.

The frenum is attached to the orifice in the scrotum, resembling a real vagina, and not like those rugose openings on the medial line which are so often found present. The labia are well formed, with a decidedly feminine smell. The color of the mucous membrane is a pale and leaden pink. No nymphae exist. The tender age of the subject prevented Dr. J. T. Taylor, of H.M. Steamship

171

Serpent, from passing probes, and menstruation had not yet taken place. The pecten is unusually large and thick; thick black curls extend in two parallel lines, fringing the parts, to the anal orifice.

It appears, therefore, that the so-called boy is a mere case of deformed clitoris, the feminine apparatus being abnormally developed. It will, however, be interesting to watch the progress of the case.

I have the pleasure to enclose a hand sketch of the original, made by me; and Dr. Taylor has kindly undertaken to forward a photograph of the parts, made by a skillful artist, the engineer of H.M. Steamship *Serpent.*

I am, *etc.*

Burton was too experienced an anthropologist to believe in the possibility of a human hermaphrodite, as he made clear in a footnote in *The Arabian Nights* (vol. III, p. 216):

Arab. "Khunsa" flexible or flaccid, from Khans=bending inwards, i.e., the mouth of a water-skin before drinking. Like Mukhannas, it is also used for an effeminate man, a passive sodomite and even for a eunuch. Easterns still believe in what Westerns know to be an impossibility, human beings with the parts and proportions of both sexes equally developed and capable of reproduction; and Al-Islam even provides special rules for them (Pilgrimage iii, 237). We hold them to be Buffon's fourth class of (duplicate) monsters, belonging essentially to one or the other sex, and related to its opposite only by some few characteristics. The old Greeks dreamed, after their fashion, a beautiful poetic dream of a human animal uniting the contradictory beauties of man and woman. The duality of the generative organs seems an old Egyptian tradition; at least we find it in Genesis (i, 27), where the image of the

Deity is created male and female, before man was formed out of the dust of the ground (ii, 7). The old tradition found its way to India (if the Hindus did not borrow the idea from the Greeks); and one of the forms of Mahadeva, the third person of their triad, is entitled "Ardhanári"=the Half-woman, which has suggested to them some charming pictures. Europeans, seeing the left breast conspicuously feminine, have indulged in silly surmises about the "Amazons."

9. Traveler's Rest

Richard Burton's return to England in the autumn of 1864 appears in some ways to have been a turning point in his life, at least so far as our purpose here is concerned. His travels were far from being at an end, his writings were as lengthy as ever; but interest in sexual practices and customs seems to have waned. Of course, he was now forty-three, and the considerable hardships he had suffered must have left some mark upon him, as must the desperate illness he contracted in his next consular post in Brazil. Also, he was now a married man; and even though he often gave the impression, particularly during the Brazilian years, of being an independent bachelor free to wander where the restlessness inherited from his father should carry him, from now on he was to spend more and more time in the company of his wife, who was determined to share whatever discomforts or dangers her husband might meet. His passion for seeing new places remained unabated, and his observation was as detailed as ever, but the focus shifted. If, in the various countries he visited, he

174

came across practices of interest to sexual anthropologists, he hardly mentioned them.

Richard Burton was to live another twenty-five years. During this period his wanderings and official postings were to take him into the Brazilian interior, to the Argentine, to Paraguay, to Peru, to Damascus, to Iceland, to the Gold Coast, to the land of Midian, and to Trieste. Long and often very dull books were to come from his pen about some of these countries, yet none of them contains material germane to this selection.

Furthermore, by none of them will he be remembered. It was not until he and Isabel had settled in Trieste that he began in earnest the work for which most of his life now seems to have been a preparation—the translation and annotation of *The Book of the Thousand and One Nights,* more generally known as *The Arabian Nights.* The footnotes that have been extracted for quotation in this book are but a minute fragment of the whole and show one aspect only of his annotations. The work was published between 1885 and 1888 in ten volumes, with a six-volume supplement. It is a monumental work in more senses than one, and of it he might well have written, with Horace, "I have raised for myself a monument more lasting than bronze."

Inevitably, he was attacked by critics, though far less vehemently than he had anticipated—indeed, the completed *Nights* was a huge success and realized a profit of £11,000. Nevertheless, Burton felt impelled to include in the final Volume x a defense of the "pornography" which the *Nights* was said to contain:

Readers who have perused the ten volumes will probably agree with me that the naïve indecencies of the text are rather *gaudisserie* than prurience; and, when delivered

175

with mirth and humor, they are rather "excrements of wit" than designed for debauching the mind. Crude and indelicate with infantile plainness; even gross and, at times, "nasty" in their terrible frankness, they cannot be accused of the corrupting suggestiveness or subtle insinuation of vicious sentiment. Theirs is a coarseness of language, not of idea; they are indecent, not depraved; and the pure and perfect naturalness of their nudity seems almost to purify it, showing that the matter is rather of manner than of morals. Such throughout the East is the language of every man, woman and child, from prince to peasant, from matron to prostitute: all are as the naïve French traveler said of the Japanese: *"Si grossiers qu'ils ne scavent nommer les choses que par leur nom"* [so uneducated as to call things by their real names]. This primitive stage of language sufficed to draw from Lane and Burckhardt strictures upon the "most immodest freedom of conversation in Egypt," where, as all the world over, there are three several stages for names of things and acts sensual. First we have the *mot cru,* popular term, soon followed by the technical and scientific, and, lastly, the literary or figurative nomenclature, which is often much more immoral because more attractive, suggestive and seductive than the "raw word." And let me observe that the highest civilization is now returning to the language of nature. In *La Glu* of M. J. Richepin, a triumph of the realistic school, we find such "archaic" expressions as *la petée, putain, foutue à la six-quatre-dix; un facétieuse pétarade; tu t'es foutue de,* etc. *Eh vilain bougre!* and so forth. To those critics who complain of these raw vulgarisms and puerile indecencies in *The Nights* I can reply only by quoting the words said to have been made by Dr. Johnson to the lady who complained of the naughty words in his dictionary—"You must have been looking for them, Madam!"

176

But I repeat, there is another element in *The Nights* and that is one of absolute obscenity utterly repugnant to English readers, even the least prudish. It is chiefly connected with what our neighbors call *le vice contre nature*— as if anything can be contrary to nature which includes all things. Upon this subject I must offer details, as it does not enter my plan to ignore any theme which is interesting to the Orientalist and the Anthropologist. And they, methinks, do abundant harm who, for shame or disgust, would suppress the very mention of such matters: in order to combat a great and growing evil deadly to the birthrate —the mainstay of national prosperity—the first requisite is careful study.

And having given the matter very careful study indeed, he proceeded, in the "Terminal Essay D," to discuss it *"sérieusement, honnêtement, historiquement"* and at considerable length, and "to show it in decent nudity and not in suggestive fig-leaf or *feuille de vigne."* (See p. 24). But in fact pederasty plays only a small part in the *Nights,* while heterosexual sex is regarded as an entirely natural passion that should be enjoyed with as much gusto as a good meal or a good wine:

The Moslem religion has no absurd shame of the natural passion. I have heard of a Persian Imam, who, suddenly excited as he was sleeping in a friend's house, awoke the master with, "I am lustful and was at once gratified by a temporary and extempore marriage to one of the slave girls. (Supplemental vol. iii, p. 33, Footnote.)

It is also very noticeable that the women in the *Nights* are prepared to enjoy the sexual act as much as the men—in fact, their demands are often greater because they delight in it so much. This was a fairly novel idea in

England in the 1880's. Some, indeed, achieved an orgasm simply through excitement rather than through penetration: for example, the Sultan's daughter who "clasped the youth to her bosom of her longing for him and fell to kissing him on the cheeks and mouth ... till her hot desire for him was quenched; though by what physical process, writes Burton in a footnote, "the author modestly leaves to the reader's imagination." He continues:

Easterners do not often notice this feminine venereal paroxysm which takes the place of seminal emission in the male. I have seen it happen to a girl when hanging by the arms a trifle too long from a gymnastic crossbar; and I need hardly add that at such moments (if only men knew them) every woman, even the most modest, is an easy conquest. She will repent it when too late, but the flesh has been too strong for her. (Supplemental vol. iv, p. 144.)

Women play such an important part in the *Nights* that Burton felt it necessary to write a brief essay on them and to contrast the position of Eastern women with that of their English and European counterparts, to the disadvantage of the latter. Since this essay was penned toward the end of his eventful life (it appears as "Terminal Essay B" in volume x of the *Nights*), it seems appropriate to quote it here.

The next point I propose to consider is the position of womanhood in *The Nights,* so curiously at variance with the stock ideas concerning the Moslem home and domestic policy still prevalent, not only in England, but throughout Europe. Many readers of these volumes have remarked to me with much astonishment that they find the female characters more remarkable for decision, action and manliness than the male; and are wonderstruck by their masterful attitude and by the supreme influence they exercise upon public and private life.

I have glanced at the subject of the sex in Al-Islam to such an extent throughout my notes that little remains here to be added. Women, all the world over, are what men make them; and the main charm of Amazonian fiction is to see how they live and move and have their being without any masculine guidance. But it is the old ever-new fable: "Who drew the Lion vanquished? 'Twas a man!"

The books of the Ancients written in that stage of civilization, when the sexes are at civil war, make women even more than in real life the creatures of their masters: hence from the dawn of literature to the present day the sex has been the subject of disappointed abuse and eulogy almost as unmerited. Ecclesiastes, perhaps the strangest specimen of an "inspired volume" the world has yet produced, boldly declares, "One (upright) man among a thousand I have found; but a woman among all have I not found" (vol. vii. 28), thus confirming the pessimism of Petronius:-

Femina nulla bona est, et si bona contigit ulla
Nescio quo fato res mala facta bona est.

In the Psalms again (xxx., 15) we have the old sneer at the three insatiables, Hell, Earth and the parts feminine (*os vulvae*); and rabbinical learning has embroidered these and other texts, producing a truly hideous caricature. A Hadis attributed to Mohammed runs, "They (women) lack wits and faith. When Eve was created, Satan rejoiced saying: Thou art half of my host, the trustee of my secret and my shaft wherewith I shoot and miss not!" Another tells us, "I stood at the gate of Heaven, and lo! most of its inmates were poor, and I stood at the gate of Hell, and lo!

179

most of its inmates were women." "Take care of the
glass-phials!" cried the Prophet to a camel-guide singing
with a sweet voice. Yet the Meccan apostle made, as has
been seen, his own household produce two perfections.
The blatant popular voice follows with such "dictes" as,
"Women are made of nectar and poison"; "Women have
long hair and short wits" and so forth. Nor are the Hindus
behind hand. Woman has fickleness implanted in her by
Nature like the flashings of lightning (Kathá s.s.i. 147); she
is valueless as a straw to the heroic mind (169); she is
hard as adamant in sin and soft as flour in fear (170) and,
like the fly, she quits camphor to settle on compost (ii.
17). "What dependence is there in the crowing of a hen?"
(women's opinions) says the Hindi proverb: also "A virgin
with gray hairs!" (*i.e.*, a monster) and, "Wherever wendeth a fairy face a devil wendeth with her." The same
superficial view of holding woman to be lesser (and very
inferior) man is taken generally by the classics; and Euripides distinguished himself by mysogyny, although he drew
the beautiful character of Alcestis. Simonides, more merci-
ful than Ecclesiastes, after naming his swine-women, dog-
women, cat-women, etc., ends the decade with the admirable bee-woman thus making ten percent honest. In
medieval Germanic Europe the doctrine of the Virgin
mother gave the sex a status unknown to the ancients
except in Egypt, where Isis was the helpmate and com-
pletion of Osiris, in modern parlance "the woman clothed
with the Sun." The kindly and courtly Palmerin of England, in whose pages "gentlemen may find their choice of
sweet inventions and gentlewomen be satisfied with courtly expectations," suddenly blurts out, "But in truth women
are never satisfied by reason, being governed by accident
or appetite" (chapt. XLIX).

The Nights, as might be expected from the emotional

East, exaggerates these views. Women are mostly "Sectaries of the god Wünsch"; beings of impulse, blown about by every gust of passion; stable only in instability; constant only in inconstancy. The false ascetic, the perfidious and murderous crone and the old hag-procuress who pimps like Umm Kulsum,* for mere pleasure, in the luxury of sin, are drawn with an experienced and loving hand. Yet not the less do we meet with examples of the dutiful daughter, the model lover matronly in her affection, the devoted wife, the perfect mother, the saintly devotee, the learned preacher, Univira the chaste widow and the self-sacrificing heroic woman. If we find (vol. iii. 216) the sex described as "an offal cast by kites where 'er they list," and the studied insults of vol. iii. 318, we also come upon an admirable sketch of conjugal happiness (vol. vii. 43); and to mention no other, Shahryar's attestation to Shahra-zad's excellence in the last charming pages of *The Nights*. It is the same with the Kathá, whose praise and dispraise are equally enthusiastic; e.g., "Women of good family are guarded by their own virtue, the sole efficient chamber-lain; but the Lord himself can hardly guard the unchaste. Who can stem a furious stream and a frantic woman?" (i. 328). "Excessive love in woman is your only hero for daring" (i. 339). "Thus fair ones, naturally feeble, bring about a series of evil actions which engender discernment and aversion to the world; but here and there you will find a virtuous woman who adorneth a glorious house as the streak of the moon arrayeth the breadth of the Heavens"

*This person was one of the Amsál or Exampla of the Arabs. For her first thirty years she whored; during the next three decades she pimped for friend and foe; and during the last third of her life, when bedridden by age and infirmities, she had a buck goat and a nanny tied up in her room and solaced herself by contemplating their amorous conflicts.

(i. 346). "So you see, King, honorable matrons are devoted to their husbands and 'tis not the case that women are always bad" (ii. 624). And there is true wisdom in the even balance of feminine qualities advocated by our Hindu-Hindi classbook the Toti-námeh or Parrot volume. The perfect woman has seven requisites. She must not always be merry (1) nor sad (2); she must not always be talking (3) nor silently musing (4); she must not always be adorning herself (5) nor neglecting her person (6); and (7), at all times she must be moderate and self-possessed.

The legal status of womankind in Al-Islam is exceptionally high, a fact of which Europe has often been assured, although the truth has not even yet penetrated into the popular brain. Nearly a century ago one Mirza Abú Tálib Khán, an Amildár or revenue collector, after living two years in London, wrote an "apology" for, or rather a vindication of, his countrywomen which is still worth reading and quoting. Nations are but superficial judges of one another: where customs differ they often remark only the salient distinctive points which, when examined, prove to be of minor importance. Europeans seeing and hearing that women in the East are "cloistered as the Grecian matron was wont ἐνσον μένειν and οἰκουρειν; that wives may not walk out with their husbands and cannot accompany them to "balls and parties"; moreover, that they are always liable, like the ancient Hebrew, to the mortification of the "sister-wife," have most ignorantly determined that they are mere serviles and that their lives are not worth living. Indeed, a learned lady, Miss Martineau, once visiting a Harem went into ecstasies of pity and sorrow because the poor things knew nothing of—say, trigonometry and the use of globes. Sonnini thought otherwise, and my experience, like that of all old dwellers in the East, is directly opposed to this conclusion.

I have noted (*Nights* 662), that Mohammed, in the fifth year of his reign, after his ill-advised and scandalous marriage with his foster-daughter Zaynab, established the Hijáb or veiling of women. [Burton points out in a footnote that the "scandal" arose not through incest, but through the ignoring of the Arab "pundonor".] It was probably an exaggeration of local usage: a modified separation of the sexes, which extended and still extends even to the Badawi, must long have been customary in Arabian cities, and its object was to deliver the sexes from temptation; as the Koran says, "Purer will this (practice) be for your hearts and their hearts." The women, who delight in restrictions which tend their honor, accepted it willingly and still affect it; they do not desire a liberty or rather a license which they have learned to regard as inconsistent with their time-honored notions of feminine decorum and delicacy, and they would think very meanly of a husband who permitted them to be exposed, like hetairae, to the public gaze. As Zubayr Pasha, exiled to Gibraltar for another's treason, said to my friend, Colonel Buckle, after visiting quarters evidently laid out by a jealous husband, "We Arabs think that when a man has a precious jewel, 'tis wiser to lock it up in a box than to leave it about for anyone to take.'" The Easterns adopt the instinctive, the Westerns prefer the rational method. The former jealously guards his treasure, surrounds it with all precautions, fends off from it all risks and if the treasure goes astray, kills it. The latter, after placing it *en evidence* upon an eminence in ball dress with back and bosom bared to the gaze of society, a bundle of charms exposed to every possible seduction, allows it to take its own way, and if it be misled, he kills or tries to kill the misleader. It is a fiery trial; and the few who safely pass through it may claim a higher standpoint in the moral world than those who have

183

never been sorely tried. But the crucial question is whether Christian Europe has done wisely in offering such temptations.

The second and main objection to Moslem custom is the marriage system, which begins with a girl being wedded to a man whom she knows only by hearsay. This was the habit of our forebears not many generations ago, and it still prevails among noble houses in southern Europe, where a lengthened study of it leaves me doubtful whether the "love-marriage," as it is called, or wedlock with an utter stranger, evidently the two extremes, is likely to prove the happier. The "sister-wife" is or would be a sore trial to monogamic races like those of northern Europe, where Caia, all but the equal of Caius in most points mental and physical and superior in some, not unfrequently proves herself the "man of the family," the "only man in the boat." But in the East, where the sex is far more delicate, where a girl is brought up in polygamy, where religious reasons separate her from her husband, during pregnancy and lactation, for three successive years, and where often enough like the Morman damsel she would hesitate to "nigger it with a one-wife man," the case assumes a very different aspect and the load, if burden it be, falls comparatively light. Lastly, the "patriarchal household" is mostly confined to the Grandee and the Richard, while Holy Law and public opinion, neither of which can be openly disregarded, assign command of the household to the *equal* or first wife and jealously guard the rights and privileges of the others.

Mirza Abu Talib, "the Persian Prince," offers six reasons why "the liberty of the Asiatic women appear less than that of the Europeans," ending with:

> I'll fondly place on either eye
> The man that can to this reply.

184

He then lays down eight points in which the Moslem wife has greatly the advantage over her Christian sisterhood, and we may take his first as a specimen. Custom, not contrary to law, invests the Mohammedan mother with despotic government of the homestead, slaves, servants and children, especially the latter: she alone directs their early education, their choice of faith, their marriage and their establishment in life; and in case of divorce she takes the daughters, the sons going to the sire. She has also liberty to leave her home, not only for one or two nights, but for a week or a fortnight, without consulting her husband; and while she visits a strange household, the master and all males above fifteen are forbidden the Harem. But the main point in favor of the Moslem wife is her being a "legal sharer": inheritance is secured to her by Koranic law; she must be dowered by the bridegroom to legalize marriage and all she gains is secured to her; whereas in England a Married Woman's Property Act was completed only in 1882 after many centuries of the grossest abuses.

Lastly, Moslems and Easterns in general study and intelligently study the art and mystery of satisfying the physical woman. In my Foreword I have noticed among barbarians the system of "making men,"* that is, of teaching lads first arrived at puberty the nice conduct of the *instrumentum paratum plantandis civibus*—a branch of the tree of knowledge which our modern education grossly neglects, thereby entailing untold miseries upon individuals, families and generations. The mock virtue, the most immodest modesty of England and of the United States in

---

*And women. The course of instruction lasts from a few days to a year and the period of puberty is feted by magical rites and often by some form of mutilation.

185

the nineteenth century, pronounces the subject foul and fulsome; "Society" sickens at all details; and hence it is said abroad that the English have the finest women in Europe and least know how to use them. Throughout the East such studies are aided by a long series of volumes, many of them written by learned physiologists, by men of social standing and by religious dignitaries high in office. The Egyptains especially delight in aphrodisiac literature treating, as the Turks say, *de la partie au-des sous de la taille*; and from fifteen hundred to two thousand copies of a new work, usually lithographed in cheap form, readily sell off. The pudibund Lane makes allusion to and quotes one of the most outspoken, a 4to of 464 pages, called the Halbat al-Kumayt or "Racecourse of the Bay Horse," a poetical and horsey term for grape wine. Attributed by D'Herbelot to the Kazi Shams al-Din Mohammed, it is wholly upon the subject of wassail and women till the last few pages, when his reverence exclaims: "This much, O reader, have I recounted, the better thou mayest know what to avoid"; and so forth, ending with condemning all he had praised. [Similarly, writes Burton in a footnote, certain Australian tribes act scenes of rape and pederasty saying to the young, If you do this you will be killed.] Even the divine and historian Jalá al-Dín al-Siyuti is credited with having written, though the authorship is disputed, a work entitled *The Book of Exposition in the Science of Coition*; my copy, a lithograph of 33 pages, undated, but evidently Cairene, begins with exclaiming "Alhamdolillah—Laud to the Lord who adorned the virginal bosom with breasts and who made the thighs of women anvils for the spear-handles of men!" To the same amiable theologian are also ascribed the *Kitáb Nawázir al-Ayk fi al-Nayk=Green Splendors of the Copse in Copulation,* an abstract of the *Kitáb al-Wisháh fi fawáid al-*

Nikáh=Book of the Zone on Coitionboon. Of the abundance of pornographic literature we may judge from a list of the following seven works given in the second page of the *Kitáb Rujú'a al-Shaykh ila Sabáh fi 'l-Kuwwat al-Báh'=Book of Age-rejuvenescence in the power of Concupiscence*: it is the work of Ahmad bin Sulayman, surnamed Ibn Kamál Pasha. [It is explained in a footnote that "Báh" is the popular term for the amatory appetite: hence such works are called Kutub al-Báh, literally =Books of Lust]

1. *Kitáb al-Báh* by Al-Nahli.
2. *Kitáb al-'Ars wa al-'Aráis (Book of the Bridal and the Brides)* by Al-Jáhiz.
3. *Kitáb al-Kiyán (Maiden's Book)* by Ibn Hájib al-Nu'man.
4. *Kitáb al-Izáh fi asrár al-Nikáh (Book of the Exposition on the Mysteries of Married Fruition).*
5. *Kitáb Jámi ' al-Lizzah (The Compendium of Pleasure)* by Ibn Samsamáni.
6. *Kitáb Barján (?) wa Janáhib (?)* [Burton confesses he can make nothing of this title].
7. *Kitáb al-Munákahah wa al-Mufátahah fi Asnáf al-Jimá wa Álátih (Book of Carnal Copulation and the Initiation into the Modes of Coition and its Instrumentation),* by Azaz al-Din al-Masíhí.

To these I may add the *Lizzat al-Nisá (Pleasures of Women)*, a textbook in Arabic, Persian and Hindostani: it is a translation and a very poor attempt, omitting much from and adding naught to the famous Sanskrit work *Ananga-Ranga (Stage of the Bodiless One, i.e., Cupido)* or *Hindu Art of Love* (Ars Amoris Indica). I have copies of it in Sanskrit and Marathi, Guzrati and Hindustani: the latter is an unpaged 8vo of pp. 66, including eight pages of most grotesque illustrations showing the various Ásan (the Figurae Veneris or positions of copulation), which seem to be the triumphs of contortionists. These pamphlets lithographed in Bombay are broadcast over the land.*

It must not be supposed that such literature is purely and simply aphrodisiacal. The learned Sprenger, a physician as well as an Arabist, says of a tractate by the celebrated Rhazes in the Leyden Library, "The number of curious observations, the correct and practical ideas and the novelty of the notions of Eastern nations on these subjects, which are contained in this book, render it one of the most important productions of the medical literature of the Arabs." I can conscientiously recommend to the Anthropologist a study of the *Kutub al-Báh.*

It must not be supposed, either, that *The Arabian Nights* is purely aphrodisiacal or erotic; nor is it, as Carlyle termed it, "unwholesome literature." It is, rather, a revelation in romance, and its magic can be more readily recognized when read in Richard Burton's flowing and erudite translation. One thing is certain: when Burton's

---

*The local press has often proposed to abate this nuisance which is most debasing to public morals already perverted enough. But the "Empire of Opinion" cares very little for such matters and, in the matter of the "native press," generally seems to seek only a quiet life. In England if erotic literature were not forbidden by law, few would care to sell or buy it, and only the legal pains and penalties keep up the phenomenally high prices.

[This contention does not appear to have been borne out by experience of recent years. Sales of *The Perfumed Garden* and of the *Ananga-Ranga* have been very large indeed. E.L.]

early brilliance as a linguist has been forgotten; when knowledge of his astonishing journey to Mecca and of his discovery of Lake Tanganyika is confined to specialist circles; when the hundreds of thousands of words he wrote about the countries in which he traveled gather dust upon library shelves, his name will still be remembered as the translator of *The Arabian Nights*.

It is possible that he might also have been remembered as the translator of erotic literature, but Isabel ruled this out decisively. In September 1890, the Burtons were back in Trieste (where he was officially consul: but no official post ever interfered with Burton's love of travel, and he let the vice-consul do all the work) and Richard busied himself with translating erotic Latin poetry and with annotating *The Perfumed Garden,* a famous Arabic work on sexual intercourse. But for him the sands were running out. On October 19th, five months before his seventieth birthday, he reached the last page of *The Perfumed Garden*: early next day he died.

There followed what has been called "the ruthless holocaust." His widow spent the next sixteen days sorting her late husband's vast accumulation of papers, burning all those that she thought might detract from his remembered achievements and reduce him in the eyes of posterity. Among these was his manuscript translation of *The Perfumed Garden*. Instead, she sought to perpetuate his memory by building for him a marble tent in a small, forgotten Catholic cemetery in Mortlake, on the southwest outskirts of London. Into this strange dwelling were laid his earthly remains, eight months after his death.

But Isabel was wrong. It is not by the enduring qualities of marble that Sir Richard Burton will be remembered, but through the monument of his written words.